THE THESIS AND THE BOOK

The Thesis and the Book

Edited by Eleanor Harman and Ian Montagnes

UNIVERSITY OF TORONTO PRESS

Toronto Buffalo London

© University of Toronto Press 1976
Toronto and Buffalo
Printed in Canada
ISBN 0-8020 6293 8

Clothbound edition published in 1976
Paperbound edition published in 1978, reprinted in 1983, 1987, 1992,
1995, 1997, 2000, 2002

Printed on acid-free paper

Canadian Cataloguing in Publication Data

Main entry under title:
The Thesis and the book

"All the chapters have previously appeared as articles in Scholarly Publishing".
Includes bibliographical references and index.
ISBN 0-8020-6293-8

1. Scholarly publishing.   2. Dissertations, Academic.
I. Harman, Eleanor, 1909-1988   . II. Montagnes, Ian, 1932-
III. Scholarly publishing.

Z286.S37T53 1987   808.02'5   C76-007893-9

This book was published in the 75th anniversary year of
University of Toronto Press, founded in 1901.

University of Toronto Press acknowledges the financial support for its publishing
activities of the Government of Canada through the Book Publishing
Industry Development Program (BPIDP).

Canadä

Contents

Contributors

FRANCESS G. HALPENNY
former managing editor of University of Toronto Press, is general editor of
the Dictionary of Canadian Biography and dean of the Faculty of Library Science,
University of Toronto

HENRI PEYRE
was for many years Sterling Professor of French at Yale University and
now is Distinguished Professor, Graduate Center, the City University, New York

ROBERT PLANT ARMSTRONG
former director of Northwestern University Press, now is professor of
anthropology and Master of College v at the University of Texas at Dallas

WILLIAM W. SAVAGE, JR
was an editor at Oklahoma University Press and now is assistant
professor of history at that university

WILLIAM C. DOWLING
was on the staff of Harvard College and now is
assistant professor of English at the University of New Mexico

OLIVE HOLMES
is editor, East Asian Research Center, Harvard University

Preface

The thesis or dissertation, prepared as part of a program of graduate study, is only rarely publishable as a book, and even more rarely as a good one. On the other hand, many books, and some good ones, have had their origins in dissertations or have been developed from research undertaken for a doctorate. The distinction between a thesis and a book is not, alas, always clear, either to the author of the thesis, anxious to secure early publication for the fruits of intensive study and laborious writing, or to some of his advisers, who may encourage the new graduate to submit his manuscript immediately for publication. The confusion arises in large part from a conflict between the traditional view that a dissertation should be publishable, and the practical imperative to produce a thesis which will convince a small committee of its writer's grasp of a restricted field of knowledge. The traditional approach to dissertations in graduate studies is criticized and defended by contributors to this volume. Nevertheless, despite all the lamentations about 'publish or perish,' publication continues to be essential for the professional advancement of most scholars, and particularly in attaining those first few vital rungs on the academic ladder.

While the author of a thesis may excusably be concerned with immediate benefits, neither he nor scholarly publishers can forget that publication has wider objectives, which include the author's own intellectual development through the criticism of his work by a broad readership of his peers. Even more important is the contribution that his ideas may make to the development of the discipline to which he belongs. What is not published, in one form or another, may be lost;

and what is published, by the same token, should be in a form and style that make it easily available to all who can use it.

The dissertation can be preserved, and reach a minimal audience, by deposit in a university library or through such valuable programs as that operated for many years now by Xerox University Microfilms. Modern technology is rapidly providing other means of preserving and disseminating the results of research. The book, however, still remains the most effective method of all for easy reference anywhere, and the contributors to this work, in their remarks, mainly imply publication in the form of conventionally manufactured volumes. Nevertheless, the advice they offer can be applied with profit whatever form of reproduction is eventually used. All their suggestions lead to one end: to make the text more eloquent, more effective, and more easily accessible to the ultimate reader.

The contributions deal with differences in the form of presentation between the average dissertation and a publishable book. The viewpoints expressed range from broad questions of purpose and style, and of scholarly editing and publishing in general, to detailed practical suggestions for rewriting. All the chapters have previously appeared as articles in *Scholarly Publishing: A Journal for Authors and Publishers*, which is published by University of Toronto Press with generous support from the Canada Council. They are gathered here in the hope that they may benefit graduate students still writing their dissertations, those who have recently earned doctorates and now are seeking publication, faculty members supervising graduate students, and all others interested in good scholarly writing.

E.H.

I.M.

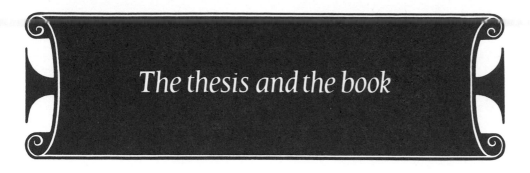

The thesis and the book

FRANCESS G. HALPENNY

A university press engaged in the publication of scholarly works is often asked whether it has a policy regarding the publication of theses. Its answer usually is that theses as such do not normally have a place in its publication program. They may do so only when they become suitable books. The following brief analysis of the difference between thesis and book will perhaps be helpful to those who are contemplating further activity with the subject of their thesis once it has been approved, and plan at some stage submission of a manuscript for book publication. It does not begin to cover all the situations that can be encountered but it will try to set forth some general principles.

To some, making a distinction between a thesis and a book may seem to be only quibbling. After all, most theses in the humanities and social sciences (and it is to these fields that the following discussion is relevant) have the same general arrangement as books: they have a table of contents, a preface or introduction, a text divided into chapters, appendixes perhaps, illustrations often, and always a bibliography. The parallel similarity of outward form may be granted, but there is nevertheless a fundamental difference in the purpose for which all these separate parts are assembled in the case of a book and of a thesis, and there is often a fundamental difference in the techniques of presentation suitable to each.

A thesis is intended to present a report of the investigation of its author into a carefully marked out segment of a topic or problem in literature or history or political science or economics or sociology. It is expected to marshal all the relevant information he has discovered in investigating this topic or problem, and so is a test of his ability to gather evidence and arrange it. Each statement he makes must be documented so that the examiners may see how he has built up his case and may judge how sound it is. The candidate is really demonstrating his ability to carry on research. The audience to whom he is demonstrating it is, of course, primarily the members of the examining committee. In addressing them he is normally expected to use a formal structure that has become the traditional format of theses.

It is only natural that, when his thesis has been approved, the author should give some attention to the possibility of its appearing in whole or in part on the printed page. Availability in the original typescript form need no longer concern him, of course, now that microfilm and interlibrary loan have assumed this responsibility. Print is a different matter, however, and a decision about how to seek it, or whether to seek it at all, requires careful thought. A gap in time of at least a few months between approval of the thesis and the author's re-examination of it with publication in mind is usually wise so that he may achieve some distance from it and therefore greater objectivity. The passage of time is well known to be beneficial in helping any author become an effective editor of his own work.

When he makes this re-examination of his thesis, the author may decide that the scope or nature of its theme does not admit of the expansion proper for a book subject or, and this is important, that he himself is no longer vitally interested in the theme and in undertaking any expansion that might be possible. If he comes to either of these conclusions, he should cheerfully decide to let the thesis rest, recognizing that it has had an honourable life and performed its task in relation to his own career, and that those who wish to consult it can do so with no great effort. It may, of course, be a source for a public lecture or a paper at a scholarly conference, or an article or two for periodicals. Good articles are always welcome and can serve perfectly well to bring the author's special contribution in his thesis to the attention of others in his field.

The author may, however, conclude that in the thesis he has had an opportunity to examine only part of a topic that challenges investigation and discussion and that he would really like to consider further with the different requirements of book publication in mind. This conclusion should sensibly be accompanied by a realization that the scope and presentation suitable for a book will likely mean a good deal more work on his part, and a determination to undertake it in the interests of his subject and his own reputation as a scholarly writer. It is also possible for an author to conclude, although he would be advised to seek confirmation from his examiners before finally making up his mind, that his thesis presents a subject in a depth and organization that would seem already suitable for a book and requires not much more than the removal of the thesis format.

The description just given will perhaps suggest the background against which most university presses have developed their procedures in relation to theses.

Experience, and the pressure of numbers in recent years, have had an important influence. It will be appreciated that it is not feasible to invite submission of all theses offered as such, when it is certain that only a small percentage of them will be close to book manuscripts at this stage and all will have to undergo revision in varying degrees. Nor would it always be in the best interests of the authors themselves for full-scale consideration of most theses to be undertaken. Readers' reports on some theses have recommended that they be converted to articles but not to books; on others they have often called for revision on such a scale as to be tantamount to the production of a new work. The obtaining of these reports inevitably used up months the author could profitably have spent in rewriting and revision before submission. After revision, the book manuscript had, of course, to go through the whole process of consideration again. Pressure on the time and concentration of press editors who consider manuscripts has also to be remembered in this connection, as well as the expense involved in the securing of the reports of editorial readers and outside consultants.

Most presses, however, would not wish to discourage sensible enquiries. What can be suggested here to authors of theses is that they will normally be able to arrive themselves, after a judicious waiting period, and perhaps in consultation with their examiners, at the decision whether or not further work with their thesis should be contemplated. If an author should decide that his thesis does warrant revision toward a book manuscript and that he can contemplate this revision with some enthusiasm, he might well sound out possible publishing interest. A good way is a carefully prepared letter, which outlines the history of the thesis (and indicates the examiners who know it), provides a curriculum vitae of the author, describes the content of the new manuscript he hopes to prepare (preferably with a table of contents), and gives a statement about the contribution to its field which he expects it to make. This prospectus would be considered by a press editor (perhaps in consultation with an outside adviser) who would then report to the author whether his house has an interest in principle in the proposed manuscript and whether it sees any value in looking at the thesis at this stage. Authors whose theses would seem to be ready for consideration as book manuscripts with not much more than technical changes might well receive an invitation to submit their work for preliminary examination in answer to their inquiry, although some independent assurance from an examiner might be sought first. Manuscripts for which the author plans a major revision, and which interest the editor, will usually be followed up by the press at the time the author has said he expects to complete his revision. Formal consideration, and a decision about publication, takes place when a final manuscript is received.

The nature of the revision so often referred to above requires some discussion at this point. There are two principal considerations to be heeded in the development of a book manuscript from a thesis. The first is the new and larger audience to be addressed and the second is the treatment of the material in the way that will best meet the needs and interests of this audience.

The new readers of a scholarly work may be imagined as 1,000 or as 5,000 in number. In general, however, whatever their number, the new readers will influence a revision in much the same way. The wider audience will, of course, include not just fellow workers in the subject, narrowly defined; many academic readers with many different interests will come to the book not because of a special interest in the writer's main subject but because what they happen to be working on or reading about touches this subject at a number of points. These readers, and sometimes others with even more general interests, will have to be persuaded to do more than pick up the book and glance at the index; the author has to think in terms of attracting their attention as he did not have to do with his small examining committee.

This challenge means that he must at an early stage answer the question how much background information he can assume in the book's audience. The answer will determine fundamentally how he must present his material. Two mistakes are possible: under-explanation (and under-documentation) or over-explanation (and over-documentation). It is never easy to find the safe and sensible course between the two; yet unless the need to attempt it is recognized, the conversion from thesis to book will be half-hearted and the result will lack force.

It is almost always true that a book prepared from a thesis requires an 'opening out' of the topic beyond the often narrow limits appropriate to a thesis. A writer for a wider public must give his topic a context. He may extend the time span of the historical movement he is covering; he may include more writers or more influences in his effort of literary criticism; or, if he is warranted in giving attention primarily to his original subject, he may support and illuminate it with a description of background that will add necessary perspective. In all this, he will aim at a manuscript that is more or less self-contained, one that does not depend on the reader's having full familiarity with an array of people, places, and events before he starts to read. The book manuscript should also lead up to the drawing of conclusions and inferences and should make judgements as it proceeds. The reader should feel that he has had the pleasure of listening to an informed person discussing a topic or a period and ordering it for his better understanding. This reaction at once suggests another most important difference between thesis and book: the difference in tone.

A thesis tends to be a formal document which has a rigid structure and is often written in 'academic' prose. Its author is not under the necessity of establishing direct communication with the reader, although he is by no means forbidden to do so. In a book there must be a sense of the author's speaking directly to his audience. This in turn involves a commitment of the author to his subject. From its opening pages a scholarly work of analysis or criticism should impart to the reader the writer's conviction that his subject is worth writing about and worth reading about. The reader should want to go on. Successful persuasion will be found, among other things, to have a great deal to do with the manner in which the theme of the book is introduced. The introductory part of a book must not only lead logically to the heart of the study but lead the reader to it, and engage him in it.

Style is another element that can do much to increase a reader's sense that he is in direct communication with the author. The indirect and carefully impersonal style often considered appropriate in a thesis can give a chill to the pages of a book. Simplicity and directness should be the aim. Jargon should be examined sceptically. The author should prefer for his sentences the active and the alive to the passive and the unduly careful. He should endeavour to introduce light and air into his prose, by varying the length and structure of sentences, by making less use of 'It is important to note ...' and 'It can be concluded that ...', by omitting formal summaries or else working them in more skilfully and informally, by cutting down sub-headings to the minimum in favour of smoother transitions in the text.

Revisions in the interest of engaging the attention of a wider audience, which may need a sketching in of background or a wider context for the topic, which will respond to a more direct address and more open style of writing, can profitably be considered also for a lecture or an article prepared from thesis material. With either one, a different audience spoken to with a different purpose creates a need for a different approach to content and presentation. A chapter taken from a thesis with only a little adjustment will rarely delight listeners or hold the attention of journal readers, however sound and original its argument may be.

Finally, a word about footnotes. These are omnipresent in theses, because they are largely the guarantees of the accomplishment of proper research. A great deal of this proof can be assumed for the purposes of a book – we do not need footnote references to well-known reference works for standard items of information about Canada, or dates and a brief biography for Voltaire when he first appears in a work of literary criticism. We do need references for quotations or for opinions with which disagreement is possible or for statements of fact presented for the first time or in a new light. All discussion of a point raised in the text should be given in the text unless there is justification for including in a footnote a remark that is genuinely – and briefly – parenthetical. A sequence of quotations from the same source running through a paragraph of text need have only one inclusive reference. The date of a newspaper editorial or of a debate in the House of Commons or the line numbers of a selection of poetry can be worked into the text and the footnote dropped. If there is to be a bibliography it can be responsible for all the bibliographical details of works cited, and the footnotes can therefore be briefer and still useful.

In making the change from a thesis to a book manuscript, there may be a great deal to do or there may be comparatively little. Nevertheless each thesis must be rigorously subjected to the questions about audience and style set forth above. In finding the right way to address his proper audience, an author may well discover that the farther he leaves his thesis behind him, mentally and physically, the better book he will write and the more people he will persuade to read it. A thesis should, in short, be a quarry from which a new structure is built.

An article bearing the present title first appeared in *Press Notes from the University of Toronto Press*, May 1962, and a second version was printed in *Press Notes*, January 1968. The author would like to acknowledge the help of Professor F. E. L. Priestley, who collaborated in the first version.

Random notes on a misunderstanding

HENRI PEYRE

University presses are a growing and much envied feature of the publishing world and of academic centres of learning in the United States, Britain, Canada, Australia, and a few other countries. They have done much to enable scholars in all fields of research to have their books published, often when such books, because of their specialized nature, might well not have reached readers in any other way. They bring out an ever-growing number of journals in the social sciences and the humanities, at scant if any profit, since few teachers and scholars can afford to subscribe to more than five or six such monthly or quarterly publications in their fields, and since the excellence of today's libraries makes those tools of information and research easily available at no cost. The editorial assistance proffered by those presses to academic authors impatient of the trivialities of punctuation marks, of references for their quotations, of clear writing, is invaluable. The exasperating if charming negligence with which professorial volumes are edited, or unedited, on the European continent stands in sharp and unfortunate contrast to the loving, and severe, solicitude with which unliberated women in the university presses, lavishing their inquisitive queries on the margin of male, hence imperfect, manuscripts, wreak their subtle revenge on would-be creative scholars. (The increasing numbers of male copy-editors are now doubtless beginning to retaliate on liberated women scholars.) University presses, on the whole generously treated by legislatures and occasionally by alumni, have ably filled a role which, in other countries, has had to be assumed by research organisms financed and run by the central government. The freedom which they have enjoyed has been unimpaired; the competition between them has proved a boon for that minority of scholarly or semi-scholarly works likely to sell over a number of years.

Still, all is not for the best in the relations between university presses and the faculties. Both the financial stringency of the seventies and the restive mood of youth, which refuses to be over-awed by the specialized publications of teachers accused of neglecting their teaching for the vanity of publishing pleasures, incite us, these days, to a revision of many of our superstitions. There is discontent in the staff of many presses with the unreadability, turgidness, unwieldy length, and occasional poverty of substance of many of the manuscripts proposed to them by professors and their PH.D.s. There is probably also the built-in grudge caused by the blatantly manifest selfishness of many professors: they reserve for the press of their own institution their specialized works, bristling with footnotes, loaded with pedantic bibliographies, replete with complacent dismissals of the out-dated achievement of their predecessors; but they are not averse to bringing out at commercial presses their financially rewarding textbooks or the now dangerously popular collections of a dozen critical essays, linked together by a hasty introduction, on one classic, which are subsequently listed under that editor's name and earn him a promotion for his 'original scholarship.'

The faculty, on its own side, has grounds for its own complaints. Regrettably, on many a campus it appears to hold, or to be held, altogether aloof from the personnel of the university press. Some professors are invited to book-launching parties, and enjoy being treated in less niggardly a fashion than they are liable to be at their own gatherings of impecunious colleagues. They pretend to admire the elaborately designed jacket of a newly produced volume or the luxury lavished on some art book intended for a Christmas gift or for collectors. But they seldom consent to learn from initiates in the humble arcana of publishing. Any young member of the editorial staff asking a prolific professor to curtail his overlong manuscript or to rid it of that precious idiosyncrasy of humanistic scholars, their privilege to be inconsistent, is looked at askance by the outraged scholar. The charge of inconsistency seems to be put forward most frequently by some charming young graduate of a women's college who must have majored in logic and insists that an older male should undertake to reconcile his diverse, or contradictory, assertions. The professor sighs with nostalgia at such a reproach: would to God his own wife, his daughters, or girl friends had evinced the same consistency in their private relationships to him! Cannot a male claim a gift of intuition now and then and, reversing the cry of Lady Macbeth, explode: 'Unsex me here!', discard masculine logic, and contend that, like all genuine creators, he has a good deal of the female perceptiveness in him?

More tact would probably be required on the two sides, and more mutual confidence. There should be a way for university presses to bring more members of their university faculties, not only into their perfunctory advisory councils, but also into their operational, editorial, and even manufacturing and commercial activities. Departments in the vast realm of the humanities would profit from inviting members of their press staff, or even of commercial presses, to give a few seminars on bibliography, on book publishing, on desiderata for a good scholarly volume, on how to edit a learned journal. Professors might well be consulted more often by editors of the presses on new trends in their fields, on topics on which new books appear to be needed, on which foreign works might profitably be translated, on which younger men at their own base or elsewhere seem to have it in them to write a timely and worthwhile volume.

Not enough editors of presses play the role of scout, perhaps out of a misplaced inferiority complex or out of excessive reverence for the aloofness of scholars who want, or think they want, to do their own obscure burrowing, digging, scribbling, undisturbed. There are many diplomatic ways of approaching even gruff and dour scholars and of eliciting useful hints from them, or even of proposing to them a subject on which they might want to write. Those scouts from an enterprising press should not too promptly take 'no' for an answer. Many a great writer, Goethe and Paul Valéry for example, has unabashedly declared that some of his work (Goethe even thought, most *great* work) was a product of occasional circumstance. So were many paintings by Tintoretto, Rubens, and El Greco, concertos and requiems by Bach or Mozart. The scholar, securely paid as a teacher, is not necessarily so penurious as an artist can be, dependent upon orders from patrons or churches. He will at first and proudly be inclined to spurn the degrading temptation: perhaps he has so little genuine originality in him that he fears losing it. Never mind. Coy maidens and stern untouchable authors have been known to entertain second thoughts after first resisting a temptation. The temptation becomes more alluring after one indulges in a few dreams or daytime reveries. The suggestion may then bear fruit. The scholar's best book might eventually come out of it. After all, it is always comforting to be assured by someone in the trade that there is probably a public, and a market, for the treatment of a timely topic suggested by an editor who should know.

All too often, such initiatives in sowing suggestions into the ears of potential authors have come, not from university presses, but from commercial ones. Naturally, the latter have more ample means at their disposal. They can afford to have representatives visit the colleges and the bookstores all over the country. In theory, if not always in practice, their firm is more eager to sell its books, hence to fill orders promptly (university presses are said to be sadly remiss on that score), to bring out a volume in paperback, to print and distribute catalogues and examination copies. Nevertheless, the time may have come for hitherto tax-exempt and timorous university presses to prove more audacious. Even if part of their operation and profit, if any, were to become taxable, the eventual gain might justify it. There would presumably be no violation of the anti-trust laws in having several university presses uniting their energies and their funds in advertising as a group, sending out emissaries as a group, and thus perhaps entering the profitable textbook trade and children's and teenagers' trade. Why should not an American university press launch, say, a Princeton or a Stanford 'Book of English Verse,' 'Book of French Verse,' 'Book of Spanish Verse,' etc., such as Oxford and Penguin did in Britain? Why not an undertaking similar to the Pelican History of Art, to *The Legacy of Islam*, *The Legacy of Greece*, and many other series long popular abroad? As things stand now, it is often the presses in Europe which organize those profitable, and highly respected, ventures, drawing upon the scholars in the United States who today make up a majority of the most competent people in many a field of economics, sociology, psychology, even of classical, English, and foreign literatures.

The reasons for the indifference of most academic writers towards their university presses, justified or not, may be listed under a few headings.

1 / Lack of aggressiveness, or merely of imaginative energy, on the part of those presses in promoting the sales of the books which they have published. Book reviews cannot be relied upon to do the task: they are much too haphazard and cursory in the Sunday supplements of our great newspapers, much too long and rambling in *The New York Review of Books*. The monthlies (*Atlantic, Harper's, Commentary*) have so reduced the space allotted to, and the interest they take in, books outside the realm of fiction or politics as to grant practically no attention to readable scholarly or semi-scholarly volumes. Communication between the achievement of the American intellectuals, now more numerous and virtually more influential than ever, and the cultured public has never yet been so poor. Yet among the three or four hundred thousand young people who graduate every year from American colleges, there should presumably be a modest proportion who have retained some curiosity about what philosophers, historians, critics now teaching or some day to teach their children, are thinking and writing. One of the truly encouraging features of our universities is the fervent hope now set in the continued reading and growing of women between twenty-five and forty who, we trust, will be welcomed into a number of professions, including the teaching one, after the period of maternity and child-raising. Is there a perfidious conspiracy of their husbands which discourages them from reading books of solid content brought out by the more fortunate males who teach, write, and, it is hoped, think on the college campuses? Teachers, including those at the graduate school level, seem to agree that there is often, in the humanities, and the arts, perhaps even in some of the social sciences and in biology, more brilliance and more depth in their women students than in the men of the same age. Is not the stunting of the resources lodged in those

feminine minds, once they leave college, one of the most revolting wastes in the development, even in the economy, of the country?

2 / As mentioned above, there has been too much passivity among the staffs of presses attached to a university, hence subsidized (even if poorly) and fairly secure in their expectation for survival. They wait for manuscripts to come to them, instead of hunting for them, nurturing the growth of a fertile idea, or approach, in an historian or in a critic, keeping informed on the promises offered by young scholars and perhaps gently guiding them. It took no superior gift of prophecy, in 1950 or 1960, to foresee that serious anthropological, sociological, and literary books about Southeast Asia, China, India, and African lands would soon be in demand and should be prompted; or books on structuralism, on linguistics, on Hesse and Beckett and Neruda; or that a reinterpretation of Greek tragedy, of the Renaissance, of Marxism, or of Freud, if accomplished with some comprehensiveness and penetration, is always in order.

3 / The manufacturing of books is expensive, and none, perhaps, is as costly as that of scholarly volumes. It so happens that the American scholar can be aided, in the course of his research, with far more substantial grants (sabbatical or research leaves, fellowships from foundations, funds provided by his own university) than any other scholar anywhere in the world. But when it comes to the publication of the results of the research thus accomplished, he meets with a rebuttal which he is bound to find unjust and wasteful. The absurd notion prevails that a serious or learned book is no different from any other product: if it fills a purpose and is 'competitive,' it should find its own market, and therefore its own promoter, or publisher. That, of course, is erroneous. But administrators will not easily be inclined to find funds for such a book; they will only very grudgingly assist their own university press to publish it. Much work of substantial merit done by American scholars today has to appear in Germany, Holland, France, or England, for lack of encouragement at home.

A similar stubborn prejudice prevails in the minds of many a press administrator. Even at the risk of publishing a book which will hardly sell, because it is priced too high, he insists that the cost should take into account all the overhead expense, plus manufacturing, designing, advertising, etc. As a result, many excellent American volumes, before or until they are reprinted in paperbacks, are priced out of the world markets. The United States, directly or indirectly, subsidizes the sale of its agricultural products abroad, even that of some of its industrial ones, shipped as foreign aid or as surplus products to lands across the seas. Yet it is not bread alone, nor, primarily, even technical knowledge or know-how, that many of the poorer nations expect from America: it is also intellectual stimulation, information on American history and politics, on the literature, the arts, the criticism in this country. Volumes of quality on, say, French literature, written by critics in the United States and published by university presses, can make a strong impression on the French, on the French-speaking Africans, on the Greeks, the Lebanese, and the Vietnamese. They help dispel the fear of American cultural imperialism and demolish the myth that the United States is good chiefly at technology, at a time when technology is repugnant to many who believe it leads to waging war and destruction. A very small fragment of the u.s. funds spent on foreign aid, not to mention on helicopters and bombs, should be diverted to enabling serious academic books to be published by university presses below cost; or to guaranteeing the buying of a sizable number of copies of such books to ship abroad. Other countries, much less wealthy than the United States, have done that; for a time and indirectly, through American money paid through the Marshall Plan. Even in Africa, Asia, South America, indeed mostly on those continents, and for a long time to come, it is through the cultured groups which read and think that the influence of the Western countries will be effectively channelled.

II

There is another side to the occasional lack of mutual understanding that can develop between scholars or scholar-apprentices eager to appear in print, over-sanguine in their expectation that their writing is so good as to deserve immediate publication, and the less than enthusiastic editorial staff of their university press which soon becomes acutely aware of their prospective authors' deficiencies. Let us confine our remarks to those scholars, old and young, whose field lies in the vast and ill-defined realm of the humanities. And let us be charitable to the old or over-ripe scholars, who are presumably beyond repair and too entrenched in their habits to attempt to redress their behaviour. The best books composed by scholars are, very often, their second or third ones, written before they reach the age of fifty and turn either sour, or superficial and repetitive, and in any case too hurried by the imposition on their time made by students, committees, lecture audiences, and administrative chores. Beyond that age, it proves difficult to remain eager enough, flexible and patient enough to undertake a prolonged piece of research, and to polish and prune a style spoiled by the redundancy and banality of lecturing. Perhaps there lies some benefit, after all, in the conspiracy of colleagues and of events which kicks ageing professors upstairs, or sideways, into a deanship, a directorship of a research institute, or some other administrative office where it is hoped that those venerable gentlemen might be reduced to silence. If they insist upon keeping their names in the public eye through more books, the directors of presses should summon up sufficient courage to explain to them that tides of taste have turned since their salad days. The most pernicious custom stems from the piety of friends of a professor-scholar recently deceased: the surviving colleagues or disciples will urge that his *opera interrupta* should be saved from oblivion and should appear with touching elegiac tributes from those whom the departed scholar once instructed. Epitaphs on graves, in older days, were less expensive, more terse, and more touching than such posthumous, often disappointing, volumes, which a press is asked to bring out in honour of a man who faithfully served the institution for thirty years.

No less embarrassing to a press must be the levity with which too many professors, having directed a PH.D. dissertation by a graduate student whom they trained, assure the young scholar that his *opus* is deserving of publication and urge him to submit it to a press. Nine times out of ten, the thesis has to be rejected by the press readers; some ill-will ensues, and not a little time and, through readers' fees and editors' salaries, money, is expended in vain. The young scholar, discouraged after having been too irresponsibly encouraged, becomes convinced that the establishment is an impregnable fortress which he cannot storm and refuses to undertake the revision, or the rewriting, suggested. Graduate studies directors and press editors should come to a meeting of minds and be made to understand each other's point of view. The faults which are blamed in almost every beginner's manuscript are common ones. They could be shunned with more candid direction from the teacher who supervises the thesis, even before the manuscript is offered to a university press. As a rule, it could be taken for granted that a PH.D. dissertation, as it is now conceived in North America, is unpublishable as it stands. Either the conventional genre of a PH.D. thesis must be altogether modified or the manuscript should be rewritten before it is presented to a broader audience than the three or four judges sitting on a PH.D. committee.

Anyone with some experience in reading theses is well aware of the deficiencies found in the very best of them; the less than excellent ones should not even be considered in an age when readers may soon become less numerous than authors and when sleeping pills lull insomniacs to slumber even more securely than the reading of scholarly prose. Excessive length, repetitiousness, exasperating slowness of pace, monotonous synopses of novels, of plays, or of earlier critical works are the most common faults in any conscientious beginner. Frequent, too, are elaborate attempts to justify the choice of the topic treated and apologetic, or cantankerous, demonstrations to the effect that, while all else concerning Dryden or Trollope or Flaubert had been considered by previous scholars, a certain obscure work or a curious aspect of the great man's output had remained inadequately noticed. Since the point has to be proved, in view of the probable questions which the candidate's committee will have to ask, the young doctor lavishes information on the work of his predecessors to show where they can be found wanting. His defensive and ponderous tactics are intended to parry all annoying questions from his examiners.

Precision is, rightly, deemed essential in a scholar's training: hence the multiplication of footnotes and references, up to several scores, at times several hundreds, for each chapter of some thirty pages. Every assertion has thus to be buttressed with evidence (as if references ever constituted evidence!), lest the young person soon to be admitted to the select company of certified scholars express an idea or a reaction which is his very own. What right has he, at twenty-five, to stand against the presumably expert view of renowned scholars from America and Europe? Impressionism is dreaded in graduate students, and enthusiasm in the presence of beauty or profundity is taken to be dangerous as leading to dreaded 'value judgements.' For two or three years, while taking seminar courses, he was supposed to read, not in order to enjoy, but to evaluate, and to discover what others had thought. He laboured arduously, piled up tiny details: he is reluctant to sacrifice them when composing his mosaic-dissertation. Like Browning's grammarian buried with honour by his disciples and, more ironically, by the poet, he will not stop until he has commented upon every minor point.

> *Even to the crumbs I'd fain eat up the feast,*
> *Ay, nor feel queasy!*

The new doctor had once to take examinations testing his 'mastery' of two or more foreign languages: he will now prove to what good use his knowledge has been put. Any quotation from Latin, German, French will be given in the original. If the eventual readers feel put off by those long quotations in foreign tongues, let them admire, or open their dictionary – or, more probably, never buy the learned volume.

But the worst sins committed by the young – and the not so young – are those of dogmatism in their approach and of obscurity in their jargonic style. In their obsession with justifying their treatment of an author on whom a dozen or more books have already been written, the new doctors select a new-fangled style and a supposedly novel approach, borrowed now from existentialism, now from structuralism, now from neo-Marxism, now from linguistics. They naively imagine that they are the sole possessors of a new magic key which opens all the locks. Fashions, however, change fast in literature, history, philosophy, or psychoanalysis, almost as fast as in molecular biology, genetics, and physics. The would-be new approach will, five years after, appear as childishly old-fashioned as the pop and op art of 1968 does in 1972. Some serene unconcern with ephemeral vogues should be among the valuable acquisitions of a humanistic scholar, supposedly dealing in permanent values.

It would also be hoped that he might address himself to a fairly broad audience of cultured persons, and not only to scholars and pedants of his own ilk. The ever-larger public composed of women and men college graduates might well, it would seem, expect to be treated with the respect that it deserves, and even courted so that it would read some at least of the books written by scholars and published by university presses. That public is potentially more receptive, less set in its constricting mental habits, more intellectually curious, than that of specialized scholars. Proust, once alleged to be difficult and now almost too clear, used to repeat that he was writing, not for critics, not for duchesses, snobs, and professors, but for the readers of a lower social rank or with a less pedantic brain, who are more sensitive to beauty and readier to share an author's new vision. In a democracy where university presses and faculties are supported by taxation and by alumni contributions, the public has some claim to being treated like adults whom academic writers might make an attempt to interest, and not like Philistines to be overawed by a terminology borrowed from rhetoric, semiotics, and other revived forms of scholasticism. The English, both in their learned journals and in their academic volumes, have succeeded in cultivating that true clarity which goes with depth and even a terse, at times humorous, elegance of prose. The French, long famous as the apostles of *la clarté française*, have, since the second world war, replaced the Germans as the perpetrators of the most turgid, needlessly abstract, high sounding, and pompously pedantic expository prose. American higher education enjoys great prestige in Europe today, for the first time in its history. It should have the courage to point the way to a return to sanity and to simplicity in style. If it does not do it, it will have missed a rich opportunity to influence other continents.

The solution to the widespread unease now experienced by publishers, readers, graduate schools, and young scholars probably lies in a drastic reform of the PH.D. degree and the abandonment of the dissertation for all young doctors at the end of their training. Very few, in the realm of the humanities at any rate, are then mature enough, expert enough as stylists, open enough on the world outside their isolated bastions, to write a valuable book at twenty-five. Like the scientists and many of the social scientists, they might be content with doing an excellent and short essay on a precisely limited topic: indeed, they do so in their graduate courses. Many of us have read students' essays, twenty or thirty pages long, which were remarkable; the same authors of those essays, however, disappointed us grievously when they attempted a whole volume. Press directors, directors of graduate studies, and deans of the most prestigious American universities might well, under the auspices of some foundation seriously concerned with the progress of American higher education, organize a symposium in which the dissatisfaction of many of us would be aired, and a constructive solution might be devised. American higher education enjoyed for several decades an era of expansion during which the number of the scholars trained and enabled to train others was of great moment. It is now entering a period of consolidation. Not the number nor the impressive ponderousness of the theses published, but the quality and maturity of a few outstanding works, is of importance. It is well known that some ninety per cent of PH.D.s in the humanities never write another work after the thesis: would it not be preferable if, having proved their fitness through other tests and through the writing of several essays of merit, the few who have it in them were incited to compose a more carefully considered and more elegantly written volume at thirty-five, instead of rushing a thesis to hasty completion in their middle twenties? A musician, a mathematician, occasionally a poet may reach his peak at twenty; an historian, a critic, a literary scholar seldom does. To the PH.D.s in literature, too lightly encouraged to get into print by their advisers, the stern admonition of one who has served as the subject, or the victim, of many a thesis, may well apply:

> *If people only wrote when they had something to say, and never merely because they wanted to write a book, or because they occupied a position such as the writing of books was expected of them, the mass of criticism would not be wholly out of proportion to the small number of critical books worth reading.*
> (T.S. Eliot, *The Use of Poetry and the Use of Criticism*, 1933)

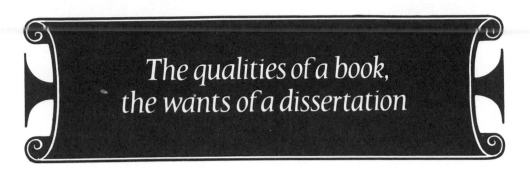

The qualities of a book, the wants of a dissertation

ROBERT PLANT ARMSTRONG

Between scholarly writers, especially new ones, and sensitive readers who demand specific qualities in the works they read, there often exists an abiding state of warfare. The reader is the aggressor and the new writer the enemy; the battleground is the editor's overcrowded desk, for the editor is the reader's ombudsman. The issue is the written page, involving clear differences of opinion concerning the level, the demeanour, and the forms of serious discourse. The discrete *casus belli* is the dissertation; and it is the chief object of this paper, in putting the issues forthrightly, to bring about the dissertation's defeat and achieve a creative discursive peace.

Pedantry has been scorned for centuries by those who, equally as serious as, if not indeed more serious than, the pedant, have ever been more humane in their work, seeking to relate the subjects of their investigations and the learned discourses which embody them to the affairs and the ends of man. In the past several generations, however, pedantry has ceased to be a subject for jest and has instead been hallowed by tradition and institutionalized. It is indeed the curse of much contemporary scholarship; but because it is a complex structure it is difficult to attack, even though it is comprised of carefully learned and utterly wretched attitudes. It has therefore flourished relatively undisturbed. Thus has pedantry been enabled to effect a qualitative jump, and instead of being a sportive vagary it has become a ponderous modus vivendi. That splendiferous emptiness men once rejected with derision, their descendants have mutated into a discursive anomaly they call the dissertation.

It is a regrettable irony – indeed even a tragic one – that the means by which a scholar in every real sense *creates* himself as scholar is so little studied, so little understood. Far from being simply 'information transference,' a book is a finite estate of being. To create such a work requires both conviction and art. The art of writing is perhaps the most important skill the scholar ought to acquire, and it ought to be the subject of faithful attention and practice. But the student does not acquire it; he learns instead the honoured forms of drab discourse, the arid niceties of documentation, and the simple-headed regimens of a proper bibliography. All that he might learn of a really profound and meaningful kind about the nature of the discourse whose exercise will be a large part of his life is relegated to accident. As a result he fails to discover the book as a viable and independent context for man.

The book is, first of all, a humane work which the writer intends to be taken seriously. That the book is humane means that its writer is at all times keenly aware that his book is *him-thinking*, and that therefore the *him* is not only ineradicable, it is the essence of the book. The best work, therefore, will be humanized by virtue of the explicit presence of an estimable man brooding through the work. That the book is humane further implies that in the final analysis its chief importance lies in its relevance to man and his estate. In the most profound sense therefore, a book, by virtue of being a humane work, is a work of human context, an existential event, a potential encounter. The humane book possesses a centre of gravity which is within man.

A book then is a fabric *in* and *of* consciousness. Now, one can hardly for a moment pretend that this distinguishes the book from the dissertation, and expect anyone to believe that the dissertation must not also have the same characteristics with respect to consciousness! What I have in mind is quite different. Since a book is a fabric in and of consciousness and since it becomes an existential context for the reader who enters into it, it follows that the book's rootedness in consciousness must be fully and richly exploited as the sub-stratum of all the rest if all the rest is in fact to be achieved. That challenge to roundedness, that wholeness which is of all attributes most subject to the critical examination of the consciousness, must be met. This requires not only all the writer's knowledge but all his fancy as well. To make *an estate* of the work – a viable and, to the probing consciousness, a veritable and existent estate – is the heavy charge placed upon the author of the book.

This view of the book is based upon many assumptions which will become manifest as we proceed. But one of the most basic tenets is an unshakeable belief that language is a human activity and that it has no more honourable function than to present man-thinking. *Man-thinking* is at every constituting moment of the book mediator between his reader and the world he perceives and incarnates into his own words. Language is a tool only in the sense that it makes man instrumental. That language is a precision instrument with its own objective existence apart from man is the premise which informs the worst dissertations – and for that matter the worst books; that it is a structure of being is the premise of the fully realized book.

A further critical feature of the book results from the model the author adopts for himself and his work. He may fancy himself as the writer of a dissertation, which is highly specialized and often therefore of little consequence, or he may regard himself simply as a writer, a certain kind of man – one who through his written prose, with serious dignity and with respect for language and discourse as a mode of being, does a human work and *establishes* an aspect of the world. Further, the writer can view his work either as a dissertation, which as a highly specialized form is also a highly restricted one, or he can regard it as an attempt at organic creation through language, different from the greatest books in the language perhaps only by virtue of the fact that it may flow from a lesser man and is devoted to less profound and stirring issues. In both these pairs of alternatives, those choices pertaining to the dissertation involve the acceptance of specialized models; the second choices do not. The writer of the dissertation sees himself as involved in the execution of a complex and erudite ritual for a cohesive, erudite, and minimal audience, and he sees his work as conforming to certain requirements of structure and levels of discourse. The writer of the book on the other hand consciously sees himself as existing within the tradition of his language and literature and regards his work as directed to every man possessed of the requisite wit, learning, and taste to appreciate it. The writer of the dissertation submits to the ritual hazing of his elders, proving to them that he has read his homework; the writer of the book rejects the indignity inherent in so foolish a demonstration. The writer of the dissertation hounds his points to the ground with packs of footnotes while the writer of books, using footnotes, when inescapable, with neither bravado nor timidity, treats his ideas and his evidence as straightforwardly and honourably as he can. He does so out of respect for his work, for his readers, and for himself, not out of a base desire to please his committee or to flatter his director.

At the outset, then, the writer must decide whether his work is to be organic or artificial, humane or academic, an end or a means, and whether he, as author, is to be civil or dull, whether he is to place himself and his work within the mainstream of the viable literary traditions of his culture or to journey the tortuous by-way of the dissertation. Further, he must determine whether he is to write a *natural* form or an unnatural one. In making up his mind on these points, the writer should bear in mind the fact that few scholars, once released from the disciplines of the graduate school, would of their own free will choose subsequently to write a dissertation. Unhappily, of course, there are some senior scholars to whom the form seems to be a natural means of expression. It is such people, one suspects, who invented the form and do the most to perpetuate it.

As a further aid to defining the book, I point to the fact that a book is in daily discourse distinguished from what is called a nonbook. Nonbooks are of several kinds; but their differences notwithstanding, they all share two common features: they tend to be written for market rather than for intellectual reasons, and they are all means rather than ends. Since their centre of gravity is external to man it is difficult, no matter what their pretensions, to regard them as humane, serious, or dedicated to creating a context in and of the full stuff of consciousness. Of all non-books, the most conspicuous example is the 'coffee-table book.' The latter usually find their market by virtue of their decorative assets rather than from any literary or intellectual merit, or for that matter – since such works are often art books – by significantly serving important aesthetic or historical purposes. Although such books are phenomena of the age of self-improvement, they seem to be of little effect, and in the final analysis they appear to serve much the same purpose as the frilly lampshades one so often sees conspicuously gracing certain front windows.

Another type of nonbook comes into being from giving expression to the desire to gather together bits and pieces of literary materials. Whether such collection is done around a common theme or around a constellation of such themes, it gives strong evidence of the simple desire to collect. The abundance of anthologies and readers attests to this. Perhaps the strength of this drive to anthologize owes much to the lucrative textbook markets, but if this is so, then in this respect we live now at a fortunate time. The abundance of relatively inexpensive paperback books seems to have ended the heyday of the big and expensive classroom reader. What-ever the case, the fact remains that the anthology is perhaps the most common form of the nonbook, and its rationale is identical to that of the coffee-table book, which appears to be that there is justification and indeed even some virtue in the snippet approach to the study of the long progress of human achievement.

There are other nonbooks which are also alien to the notion of book as humane, though these, by and large, are without attractive markets, thus making the motives for their compilation less comprehensible. I have in mind both the symposium and the festschrift. At their worst, these two nonbooks are empty forms of flattery; and even though at their best they may constitute major contributions to knowl-edge, yet publishers have grown wary of them. Like the coffee-table book, some symposia and festschriften are dedicated to vanity; like the anthology, their parts are often disparate; like both, they are in general mundane and without interest to any save the specialist with a marked tolerance for the dull, the inane, and the incon-sequential. Still, both the festschrift and the symposium are published, even fairly bad ones. Vanity and the amazing support vanity can generate sometimes constitute so powerful and insistent a force that the publisher finds it difficult to resist; he accepts the work unenthusiastically, and brings out a small printing.

There are more profound traits than market and vanity, however, which the genres of nonbooks have in common, and these are the features which perhaps distinguish them most significantly from the book. The coffee-table book is likely to be deficient in thoughtfulness and in coming to grips with a problem, though it may be both synthetic and programmatic. The anthology often rates somewhat higher in thoughtfulness but again fails to grapple with the issue. The symposium and the festschrift at their best can exhibit thoughtfulness and thoroughness, but common emphases, perspectives, values, and judgements are absent.

In short, nonbooks are marred by the absence of probity, of unity, and of responsibility. Each of these terms, save perhaps responsibility, is clear enough. *Probity* designates that quality of being at once both significant and illuminating, and *unity* is the coming-togetherness of the work into a whole. *Responsibility* is in one respect the obligation to treat the subject in the fashion it deserves, which the word ordinarily means. But it implies more than this, for the proper way of treating a subject is thoughtful, analytic (or synthetic), programmatic and exhaustive, fully rounded, taking hold of a problem. Works so treated achieve that marvellous three-dimensionality characteristic of the good book. Each of these three terms – probity, unity, responsibility – is an important criterion of the book and must be present; if one or another is absent, a nonbook results.

The dissertation may lack any or indeed all these characteristics; thus it is clear that the dissertation is another genre of the nonbook. It is in all probability for failure to honour the criterion of probity that dissertations most commonly fail to be books. The dissertation never achieves that quality of being historically, socially, conceptually, aesthetically – *humanely* – significant. The reason does not lie solely in the fact that the writer has written a dissertation instead of a book. There are some writers who deserve no greater challenge than the dissertation. I am concerned here, however, rather with that person who could achieve probity but who is precluded from doing so by the requirements of a system committed to a form to which probity is alien – because the work is usually carefully kept minimal, cut off from any but the most apprentice-like intellectual pretensions or achievements. Its mass is thus limited, and it is dedicated to embodying certain conventions of purpose and procedure.

The dissertation is likely, under even the worst of circumstances, to exhibit some unity of concept, owing to the fact that phenomena have been selected, an inquiry conducted, and data organized in relation to the 'problem' which is the core of the dissertation. But it is the rare dissertation that does not fail when it comes to unity of address. 'Address' involves a complex of factors – the strategy compounded from both the consideration and the demonstration of the question; the attitude toward the subject of the work as well as toward its hypothetical readers

facts and views of predecessors and to range creatively and with confidence over the domain.

In the best books, there develops from this freedom a sense of urgency which seldom blesses the dissertation. It comes also from the prerogative allowed the author under such circumstances to presume both his own authority and the importance of his work. This, then, is the second element in that cluster of secondary characteristics that distinguish the book.

A third item in this cluster is the presumption of the value of the expression of one's self when defining an idea, a judgement, or a fact. At the same time, this presumption entails the recognition of the privilege of invoking and making operative this value. It stresses recognition of the importance of one's self as ground for one's views, thus opening to the author the opportunity to engage on that voyage of simultaneous self-discovery and phenomenon-discovery which provides the foundation for his presumption of the importance of his work and his presumption of authority. The implicit assumption in the writing of a book is that the author himself is important. The assumptions concerning the writer of a dissertation, it need hardly be said, often appear to run quite contrary to this view. This presumption of the importance of one's self to the inquiry, besides having profound ontological implications, has more readily apparent and exceedingly attractive consequences as well, for it permits the expression of the writer's own personality in his prose to the limits of his ability to work in the language.

I am writing here about the worst dissertation and the best book. But not all books, not even all good books, are of the kind I have been discussing. While the book which is humane, which establishes a significant human context, which in roundedness and credibility creates a field of consciousness – extending the reader's consciousness by adroitly, trenchantly, and creatively directing it toward new phenomena or to new perspectives on old ones – is in my judgement the best book, its number represents perhaps but a small percentage of the books published each year. Most works are either aimed in the same direction as the best book, but are notably deficient in some respects, or else they are of a quite different sort. The book we have discussed so far is the thesis book. There is also, however, the non-thesis book, and many terminal graduate discourses are likely to be of this type for the plain reason that it is in most respects an easier kind of project to undertake.

The thesis book is primarily creative, establishing through originality of concept and argument a position which has not previously existed or is not generally accepted. A non-thesis book, on the other hand, is content to describe or to explain that which already exists. Non-thesis books are exemplified by some archaeological studies and certain histories and biographies, which are intended to do no more than record the verifiable events of the life of a period or of a man. Now we know as a matter of fact that no presentation of history or biography proceeds without selection and that that selection invariably betrays the presence of value as a principle of selection. This value is a point of view. The non-thesis book therefore is one which, while it is indubitably written from a point of view, yet exists within an unquestioned intellectual tradition and does not specifically argue a case or offer distinctively new or importantly modified points of view. The non-thesis book is inherently conservative, and the non-thesis dissertation is the safest kind of dissertation to write.

The ontological nature of the non-thesis book is as unlike that of the thesis book as a photograph of Cézanne is different from one of his self-portraits. The non-thesis book is a sketch or a profile of what incontestably exists; unlike the thesis book, it does not have as its objective the establishment of an aspect of reality. The only structures the non-thesis book must incorporate are the immanent ones of the phenomenon or process with which it is concerned, as these structures are traditionally accepted to be, within the author's own tradition. By definition, therefore, there is unlikely to be any major disputation over the nature of those structures or their interrelationships or their significance. This is not to say that there may not be scalding controversy over the details as represented. But unless the whole premise of observation is rejected by virtue of an opposing thesis, this controversy is certain to be restricted to a question of the adequacy or the reliability of the account.

So much, then, for a brief overview of the most striking inherent differences which distinguish the book from the dissertation. But there are other distinguishing factors which are not inherent but which often – even though extraneous – have a determining influence upon the work, for they can be insidious and insistent. They amount to a concerted power which often prevents the young scholar from producing a book in his first extended job of professional writing. Wholly external to the writer, this power is the combined product of tradition, the nature of graduate education, and the role and personality of the dissertation director. Tradition has it that rather than being the first act of the scholar, the dissertation is the last act of the student. The dissertation is viewed therefore as the work not of a professional but of a pre-professional. Thus the writer of the dissertation is forced by tradition to resort to the writing of a form that is dysfunctional, because in its primitive form the dissertation will be read by few and because no publisher will in all probability consider publishing it as it stands. At the same time, tradition places a great value upon publication, with the result that the young writer finds himself caught in a vise between forces, being required to remain a student, presenting what often amounts to little more than an underwrought and overextended term paper for his dissertation, and at the same time being required to publish as a means of advancing his professional career.

The agency of tradition is the graduate school which, after the model of the rest of the university, treats the graduate student as student. The graduate school seldom conceives of its scholars in any way profoundly different from that in which undergraduate schools think of their freshmen students. It therefore permits the perpetuation of tradition by approving the research of a trivial proposition and its incorporation into what, in the world of 'real' communication, can only be called a dysfunctional form. We may consider ourselves blessed that there is, here and there, some evidence of the weakening of this system. At one university recently the PH.D. candidate, having been examined on his research, was discharged with the degree promised and no dissertation required. He was instructed rather, and quite simply, to produce a book based upon his research. The system that generally prevails, however, is but another instance of the great pains American society takes to postpone the maturation of its young.

There is every reason why, in this day of PH.D. overproduction, the requirement to write a dissertation should be dropped and the requirement to write a book substituted. Such an action might impede PH.D. production, enrich scholarship, take young scholars in the serious terms the great majority of them deserve, and give them early acquaintance with that viable form of communication they will use throughout their productive lives. There can be little doubt that this more creative and worthwhile use of human energies would constitute its own reward. In addition the economics of learned book publishing, which militate against the publication of the dissertation owing to its negligible market and the subsequent high cost of publication, would be affected, I believe for the better, in view of the fact that labour would be saved and better and more marketable works would eventuate.

Under some circumstances, such as the presence of an intellectually imperialistic director of research, one of the worst faults of the dissertation is perpetrated. In the good dissertation, as in the book, the genetic principles of the work's growth are inherent in the field, the thesis, the data, the inquiry, and above all the writer. But in the unfortunate circumstances provided by the aggressive director, the genetic principle is an external one. Instead of conducting research after his own interests and in his own fashion, the student investigates some minor area of the research director's field of interest. His research thus becomes but a footnote to the research of his professor, and the sole achievement may well be only that the senior man will not have to conduct some research for which he himself had little time and perhaps even little inclination. Under such circumstances there is practically no possibility of a book, and the whole project of the dissertation, once the degree has been granted, had best be broken down to some simple stage at which the parts may be studied, reassembled, and permitted to grow after their own dictates, perhaps into one or two papers. Inevitably and wastefully some large part of the work will have to be abandoned.

If the writing of dissertations is to be discouraged and the writing of books encouraged, it is obvious that profound changes must come about in the requirements for graduate degrees. The graduate schools must revise their ideas and expectations regarding that major writing project upon which the awarding of the degree in large measure depends. Further, steps must be taken to insure the complete intellectual freedom of the candidate, perhaps by distinguishing his research director from his dissertation director. As an added step it might be well, as often as possible, to include a professional editor as a full member of the candidate's committee.

All that is wrong with graduate school writing as it tends to be practised today is symbolized by the existence and extraordinary popularity of *A Manual for Writers of Term Papers, Theses, and Dissertations* by Kate L. Turabian (University of Chicago Press). While undeniably useful within its limited terms, this manual, in wide use among dissertation writers, makes no mention of the fact that the dissertation is, or ought to be, a form of discourse. On the contrary, sole attention is given to the mechanics of presentation. That this is so reflects the staunch prevailing attitude toward the dissertation, namely that it is not expected that the doctoral research or the extended statement of that research and its arguments will be of consequence. All that matters is that the work be written in a scrupulously traditional fashion. Footnotes, most often the curse of the dissertation as far as the publisher is concerned (for they are overused to the point not only of vice, but, worse, to utter dependence of mind), are treated in thirty of the manual's 103 pages – an amount considerably greater than that directed to any other topic. In contrast, the discussion of the physical presentation of the body of the text itself is accomplished in twelve pages. While on its own terms the manual is reliable and beneficial, its existence without the concomitant existence of another manual devoted to those vastly more important dimensions of the thesis in terms of its nature as an achievement in extended and serious discourse is profoundly revealing. The attentions of the writer must early be fixed upon the humane and genetic nature of the book as the consummate form of mature discourse.

The dissertation's deadly sins

ROBERT PLANT ARMSTRONG

The dissertation system must have laid at its door an enormous squandering of creativity, youth, time, and money each year upon the execution of prose works that do not communicate significantly and are therefore dysfunctional. The publisher, upon whom depends much of the scholar's success, usually refuses even to look at them. The system, the dissertation director operating within it, and the writer contingent upon both all conspire to commit six grievous assaults upon discourse – sins, indeed, which alienate the writer and his work from that state of intellectual grace whose outward sign is serious, straightforward, responsible, and skilful communication. These assaults are amateurism, redundancy, trivialization, specializationalism, reductionism, and arrogance. One or all of these defects can usually be found in any given dissertation.

AMATEURISM

By regarding the dissertation as a pre-professional piece of work, the graduate school postpones its students' maturation and encourages in them contentment with amateurishness and unprofessionalism. Under the existing system, the writer of a dissertation has only limited opportunity to develop any real sense of his role in the field of his studies. In what is in all probability the major intellectual enterprise thus far in his life as a scholar, he is accordingly held back by a sense of his own lack of worth. Within all but the hardiest this intolerable ambiguity results in debilitation of energy, enthusiasm, and resolve – buttressed by a biting and visceral sense of frustration. He is both intellectually and emotionally unprepared to undertake the task of writing for which he has no option. Professionally the student is without locus, and personally he is without a sense of fixity. Small wonder then that his control over whatever form he chooses may be less than sure. And if his prose is unexciting, he is at least playing safe. If his work is part this and part that – part pre-professional and part professional – it reflects what he himself is at the time of writing.

A second characteristic of the system makes his situation even more hopeless, insuring the lack of confidence and competence which produces amateurishness. For the writer is expected to undertake a caricature of learned discourse whose sententiousness intimidates him (perhaps it revolts him as well) and whose artificiality of form and rhetoric arouses hostility in anyone who has read real books and responded to that naturalness of structure in prose which is characteristic of the world beyond the seminar room.

Artificiality of form was perhaps more noticeable in the dissertation a decade ago than it is now, although one still encounters dissertations built upon the older model of 'statement of the problem, review of the literature, body of the dissertation, and a conclusion which must be more than a simple summary of what has preceded it.' At the very least this prescription creates a tiresome sameness in dissertations; at the worst it destroys the subtle plasticity which is required to set forth ideas effectively.

Artificiality of form is found today chiefly in the lingering propensity of dissertation directors to demand the inclusion of irrelevant demonstrations. Such demands inhibit the first-rate student's drive toward the clean, simple, direct discourse which leads immediately and resolutely to the point, along the path of least conceptual and formal resistance. The new writer, under the worst of directors, is carefully taught discursive obfuscation and dishonesty; under some others he perhaps learns only a slight dissembling; and under the best, no dishonesty at all. But too often straightforward thinking is stultified by methodological, conceptual, and informational prolixity.

Artificiality stems also from the dissertation's unspoken rules of rhetoric. That so few bad principles can generate such vast volumes of bad prose is hardly to be believed. The first of these principles is the cowardly conditional, by which dissertation writers remove themselves from the need to state a forthright fact in a forthright mood. I suspect that the dissertation uses more conditional sentences than does any other prose form in the language. The worst offenders in this respect are the social scientists. In these disciplines the young appear to learn early in their careers an inviolable relationship between truth and tortuous conditionality. Thus: *all things else being equal, it would appear to be the case that, under given circumstances, it may not be uncommon for writers of dissertations to execute certain prose styles which those who seem to like their English straight and strong might conceivably call a perversion of the language.*

The pusillanimous passive is a second characteristic of dissertational rhetoric. Its popularity is rooted in a notion that assertions in the passive voice are not only less forthright, but somehow also more objective than those with an active verb. But over-use of the passive robs prose of its vitality, and reduces it to a namby-pamby mishmash of inconclusiveness. The assumption that the passive voice lends objectivity is clearly nonsensical: *it is to be hoped that the use of the passive voice which is resorted to by writers of dissertations, to whose mastery of it is attributable reams of pages offensive to the educated ear, will be somewhat more markedly attenuated.* As this example indicates, outlandish diction makes its own contribution to the amateurishness and barbarism of dissertation prose. When these three faults are forged into a common fabric, the effect is frightening.

The dissertation's amateurishness further reveals itself in pedantry and cowardice. The former is most notably manifested in servility to that convention which forbids the author to say anything on his own, plaguing his reader instead with a footnote to nearly every fact and opinion. I am confident that someone, in referring to the earth's roundness, must have documented the assertion with a reference to Esdras and Columbus.[1] The basis of this slavery to footnotes is the same insecurity which produces the cowardly involutions of style. Nor need it stop there. From playing safe with facts and prose, the student passes to playing safe with concepts, and thus loses probity.

Amateurism produces an unreadable, passive, and largely insignificant dissertation. That it derives in considerable measure from the system itself, from the writer's commitment to an unnatural form, does not alter the fact that an amateurish dissertation is one of the most monumental, lamentable, and stupid wastings of human intellect and energy to be found in the whole spectrum of our culture.

REDUNDANCY

The six defects of the dissertation are not neatly separable. They are closely related and interdependent. In defining redundancy as that condition of discourse in which there is more prose than information, we must not therefore be surprised to find several of the qualities already discussed under amateurism.

Redundancy is of two kinds, structural-functional and informational. The first appears in such structural elements of the dissertation as the review of the literature, which add little to our understanding of the author's thesis. If we conceive of structure itself as important in the progressive advancement of the thesis, then anything which fails to contribute to that forward movement, such as the review of literature, is anti-structural. Then there are other elements of structural redundancy – reviews of arguments which require no reviewing, extended excursions into methodology first because this is expected and then as an exercise for its own sake, slavish use of footnotes which are non-functional save to fulfil the expections of those who work the system, and dysfunctional rhetoric as described above.

By informational redundancy I do not mean that a given reader may already know the details of the field in question; that is a function of the experience and knowledge of the individual. Rather, informational redundancy comes from the common dissertational practice of citing the obvious. This is nothing but a demonstration for the benefit of those who, by virtue of their rank, no longer have to practise it themselves. Unfortunately, it is a worse than pointless exercise. Any effective informational element makes a distinctive contribution to the work in question. But in the dissertation, accepted theses are demonstrated and redémonstrated; time-honoured techniques are employed to their exhaustion and the readers' surfeit; redundant charts, tables, and diagrams are not only provided but discussed at length; subsidiary problems are explored which take us far afield from a tight and persuasive consideration of the argument. Redundancy weakens the surface tension of the work: it vitiates the density of information while maximizing the verbiage. The making of points has natural limits which the careful and sensitive writer perceives but which novices often miss.

TRIVIALIZATION

It is depressing to think that the ultimate discourse in a program of graduate studies can be trivial – and indeed frequently is. But one may as well face up to the fact that a dissertation which is trivial is so *basically*; its triviality is irremediable. About all one can do with such a manuscript, aside from simply letting it rest undisturbed, is to extract from it an article or two for the more dogged and moribund of the learned journals. Indeed, this is precisely the advice publishers usually give the writer, who too often makes his overture with more-than-merited optimism and insistence.

Many an editor concludes that the triviality of dissertations does not wholly derive from the tradition of graduate education or the nature of the work but, to be blunt, from the triviality of the writer's mind. But triviality is not always an exposure of the author's inner reality. One is often aware of the presence, lurking behind the dissertation, of a working mind bigger than the concepts and data in which it has been entrapped. One suspects that the writer has been victimized – by an accident of selection, by an uninspiring *milieu*, by poor advice, by the confidence game of his dissertation director, or by that director's personal triviality of mind. (It is only fair to balance the record by noting that excellence in works written for the degree often results from excellence of supervision.)

Trivialization thus can stem from restrictions on the writer – to a topic in which he has little interest, if any at all, or to an aspect of the topic which is not as rich, challenging, or seminal as others which he is competent or disposed to deal with. In both cases trivialization may result from the writer's hireling attitude. It may also result from the writer's lethargy. He can, as the experiences of some writers show, tailor his thesis – even if it was originally framed broadly and excitingly – to fit his data so that his dissertation is a neater package but of less consequence. In fairness it must be added that such tailoring may also occur after vigorous and exhaustive research. If the data *cannot* adequately support the thesis, the writer can only either abandon the work, which is often not feasible, or else revise the thesis to fit what data are available.

Trivialization occurs, finally, when the writer fails to perceive fully the implications inherent in his research. More often than not, however, this failure is to be attributed to the next sin.

SPECIALIZATIONALISM

This is a word which was expressly created to possess the heuristic value of embodying what it names – an insensitivity to language on the one hand, and to considerations of audience on the other. *Specializationalism* bears to *specialization* the same relation that *scientificism* (or *scientism*) bears to *science*.

It is inevitable that a dissertation should be specialized. But the question is whether in fact specialization with its concomitant limitation of communication does not sometimes become an end in itself. Specialization usually minimizes the audience. The dissertation does this efficiently, since it most often remains forever unpublished, with an audience restricted to the author's most loyal friends, his examining board, and those few determined fellow-specialists who secure it either from the library of deposit or from University Microfilms. For works of such limited interest, the access provided by the latter institutions is wholly adequate.

But exclusion by means of ardent specialization can derive from more than the *nature* of the topic under investigation. There are two less natural causes – the rhetoric and the adamantly restrictive nature of the dissertation. We have perhaps devoted enough attention to the rhetoric. Let us define simply what is meant by 'adamantly restrictive nature.' I have in mind here the strong inclination of dissertation writers and directors rigorously to avoid generalization beyond the thesis itself and such 'hard evidence' as has been adduced to support it – even when it is perfectly clear that implications beyond the thesis and its data are present and clearly formulable. If, for example, a conclusion of moment to historiography is inherent in the study of a minor Renaissance court figure, or to social theory from an anthropological inquiry, to the social sciences in general from an economic study, or to the humanities from a sociological study, then why not – in the name of sanity – follow where the opportunity to generalize leads? It is likely that viewing the thesis in the broadest terms possible will give it greater value than either the writer or the director had ever thought likely. It is equally likely that its publishing history will not end in a half-dozen rejections and profound auctorial despair.

REDUCTIONISM

The tendency to write about a part of a process, object, or event as though it were the whole of the phenomenon under study is, of course, reductionism. To believe that the reduction is reflective of reality and to act in terms of it – and to urge others to act in terms of it – is arrogance.

It is true that one cannot in every instance study *all* of any given phenomenon. Writers realize this; so do research directors. Even editors realize it. But to pass from the modesty of this perfectly reasonable position – because it may not fire one's imagination or appease one's megalomania – and to maintain that one *can study* and indeed *has studied* all that is relevant of a process, object, or event, by means of a model, and thus to accept that model as real in its own terms, is an act of intellectual fraud. Yet this is precisely what is done, rampantly, in the humanities and the social sciences. To encourage it is shocking in disciplines avowedly dedicated to the study of man-in-the-world, which in theory at least espouse the multiplicity, the subtle and elusive complexity, and the protean inexhaustibility of man's acts of being, his objects, and his events.

Reductionism is not, alas, the kind of defect which prevents a work from being published. It has been in fashion for the past few decades, and has been eagerly looked for and issued by both commercial houses and university presses. There is rich evidence, however, to indicate that its popularity is dwindling, and we may all look forward to a more honourable time when man's models are recognized in terms of their limitations and are not made the measures of all things.

Yet doubtless reductionism of a more insidious sort will continue to infect dissertations – born not of philosophy, nor even of perversity, but rather of ineptitude and inexperience. This is the reductionism of bumptiousness and stupidity. Whether cunning or clumsy, it trivializes both the world and man. It is so outstanding that it deserves its own category in this list of cardinal defects.

ARROGANCE

This is the error defined above, and it is of two kinds – the arrogance of those who know they are being arrogant, and the arrogance of those who don't. The arrogance most likely to suffuse the dissertation is of the latter kind – brassy, and without that virtuosity which sometimes accompanies conscious exploitation (for in the hands of a genius arrogance may have an *élan* that compels admiration).

I shall leave the anatomy of arrogance in general to moralists and others con-

33

cerned with the diagnosis and improvement of the human character. In the dissertation, it manifests itself as a haughty resistance to change. A book can be hospitable to arrogance: it can be personal and can even, indeed, be dedicated to setting forth a banquet of piquant and enticing displays of the author's vintaged self-estimation. But a dissertation is not personal. It is supposed to be dedicated to the exposition of a thesis which is, in some sense or to some extent, true in direct relationship to the degree to which it is removed from the personality of the writer. Obviously, resistance to change on the part of the author can be inimical to the best realization of such a work.

If the dissertation is accepted for revision and publication, it is in the editorial revision that the serpent of arrogance usually bares its fangs – at the first attempt to suggest improvement. By and large, editors are accustomed to the juvenescent tantrums of neurotics. But one can hardly blame those who now and again acquiesce in rage, yielding to the temptation to permit a particularly difficult author wilfully to commit an idiocy in print. They rightly argue that he may as well be perceived in more than one aspect of his true self.

1 / *Encyclopedia Britannica* (Chicago, 1971), vol. 6, p. 111.

Revising the dissertation and publishing the book

ROBERT PLANT ARMSTRONG

Revision is not a quick rerun, a comma added here or deleted there, a bit of finishing up. As anyone who has attempted it knows, revision is a process – the process of bringing things to rights; and those who have tried it know that it is arduous, and as creative and demanding as the production of the nearly always abortive first draft. A book evolves for months, for years even, some aspect or stratum or face always in motion, becoming that which it is not yet but shows it may become. Revision requires both the ability to perceive what is unfulfilled and the energy and cunning to bring about the fulfillment. It is thus quite another process than that attention to detail which is beguiling because so easy, and which, while essential, can always, as profound and genetic matters usually cannot, be done with the help of a good editor. Revision works sea-changes in the book that none but the work can define and none but the creator himself can perceive and bring about.

At the same time, however much a virtue revision is, it has its defect as well. The defect of revision is *constant* revision, where revision becomes neurotic and preventive instead of creative and liberating. An editor who encounters this neurosis should seek escape, for the neurotic writer tries to put the editor on a string: the wary editor declines to participate in so sterile a relationship.

The neurotic reviser may be the author of one of three types of works, which I shall call the security book, the insecurity book, and the messianic book. Perpetual revision of the first type is necessary because it is only by virtue of the work's being ever incomplete that the author can avoid facing the judgements of his peers and possibly being found wanting. The writer of the insecurity book on the other hand must ever postpone completion of his work because of new research he must take into account. Like any neurotic he is a genius at discovering such evidence as will support his inaction. Naturally, he often becomes enormously learned in the process and becomes a valuable asset to his university even if he doesn't publish. The writer of the messianic book is in a somewhat similar state. For him the time is not yet ripe (rather than the book); he is confident he is on the verge of discovering a principle or formulating a generalization which will restructure his discipline and earn him the fame for which he has so long waited. The writer of the messianic book is, furthermore, doubtful whether any publisher has the perspicacity to comprehend or value it fully.

Once in a great while a foolish editor or colleague will pry loose from its author the messianic book, or the insecurity book, or the security book. When this happens, both editor (or helpful colleague) and author will live to regret it. The editor discovers his nemesis – the author who is forever changing his text, who quibbles over design, and who visits all his frustrations upon his editor. What is more, upon publication of the book the author often finds his worst suspicions justified – the book is ill received and he hates himself, his colleague, his reviewers, his editor, his publisher, and the system. Far better he had spent the rest of his life revising.

Yet *revision* is a marvellous word. It means re-seeing the work; and the *-vision* part of it suggests more than mere seeing. 'Vision' can connote perception of the ideal and imply a marvel. Thus revision may truly be called a marvellous word. It is also an optimistic word, for to re-vision the work and shape it more closely towards the ideal attests to the viability of the creative principle in *homo faber*. At the same time, *revision* is elusive, for it is unique with each writer confronting his first draft. It is as profound a process as he is profound, as subtle as he is subtle, and therefore, inscrutable. Thus no program of simple or even difficult steps can be described in working a revision. It is possible, however, to make a few observations which generally apply.

Some of the aspects of revision can be discussed under the rubrics of the three prime virtues of the book: probity, responsibility, and unity.

REVISION FOR PROBITY

The basic concern of the writer of the dissertation (having won his degree) is to ascertain whether in fact he has been developing the proper thesis, for the thesis which met the requirements of the dissertation may not be at all adequate for the book. The thesis director may, indeed, have shunted the author into an alternative and less important path. Now the writer has the chance to revise his work, to reinstate his original thesis and eliminate the one incorporated into the dissertation for the purpose of securing a PH.D.

But the real thesis can be lost in other ways or it may be that the writer never found the thesis he should have been asserting throughout his inquiry, in which event even after revision a bad book will result, if any book results at all. It may be the author's own obtuseness that occludes the probity and authenticity of the work. Or he may have succumbed to one of the tyrannical conceptual fads. Whatever the cause, the result is the same: a potentially meaningful work is aborted.

The author is probably fortunate, if hardly laudable, if he has consciously perverted his thesis for pragmatic ends. Under this circumstance revision is relatively simple. Otherwise, finding the hidden thesis – or, even anterior to that, discerning that there is a crypto-thesis – can be difficult. In any event, given that the dissertation is based on an inapposite thesis, the first and most important job of revision is to identify the right one.

If the author did not wilfully misdirect his dissertation, there is a strong possibility that he will not recognize that he has the wrong thesis. Yet such a writer may not be hopelessly lost – he may merely require the slightest lead in order to extricate himself fully. The moral is obvious: even if one thinks his work ever so good, the candid opinions of those whom he respects are of value. Candid opinions are, however, rare.

A trial separation of the writer from his work (a final divorcement often happens at this point) is essential under all circumstances. Then a leisurely return is in order, reconstructing the work in one's mind, playing with the thesis as a conceptual sport, testing it for fullness and further applicability. Finally, the writer distances the dissertation from himself so that he can look at it dispassionately, and make an uncompromising evaluation: how does this work compare in weight and significance, in probity, with the important theses of the discipline, and, if it fails to measure up, is it true that the work is negligible or did it somehow drift into inconsequentiality through misdirection, lethargy, lack of control, absence of ability, or the sway of fashion? At this point it is perhaps well to examine the progress of the work, from beginning to end, in order to see if it is possible to gain hold of any loose ends, or pattern of loose ends, which will lead back to that confounding of errors which has grown into major misdirection, a misdirection which has through its ever-compounding course created a different work. Indeed, if at any point a clever argument has taken over from the author – which is a much less mysterious occurrence than it might seem – let him be deeply suspicious.

The identification of the right thesis can proceed by such methods of triangulation. When the sensitive writer – and it is 'sensitive' which is the ineluctable term in these formulations – sights the lost thesis he will feel a shock of recognition that reverberates with unmistakable authority.

The most basic task of revision is this recognition; all else depends upon it. The other points to be considered are, however, important, because they maximize the values implicit in good work.

We have noted that revision is a process. For that matter a book is itself a process, and so must its chief virtues and aspects be. Probity is a process and as a process it exists in time. As a temporal continuum it is subject to dynamics, and it is in the various modulations of the work that revision can be most creative and rewarding.

Pertinence, consequence, and seriousness of purpose must be ever-present in the work, but they need not pervade it with maximum intensity. A book pulsates, it has systoles and diastoles; from these we infer its vitality. The book's pulses derive from alternate intensifying and relaxation of the three aspects of probity. Like a man, the book grows more intense and more serious, and its acts become of greater consequence and pertinence as it draws nearer to critical points. And like a man under such circumstances, its breath comes faster, its whole physiology is speeded up. This variation of pace and this modulation can be achieved by the writer in the process of revision. Herein lies his artistry. His sensitivity – heightening his knowledge, giving it an affective dimension – his own imagination, and his skill to plot and execute the dynamics of probity he perceives are his sole allies in bringing the work to life.

The dissertation will require more and more arduous labours in pursuit of these simple dynamics than will the work which was written in the first place to be a book. At the same time, it is the abashed writer of the dissertation who will be most bewildered by this advice. It would be easy to warn him not to try, but as a publisher I know well that that talent which takes longest to burst into flame sometimes finally burns the brightest. Therefore I can but advise him to read the best writers of his discipline and his day with an awareness tuned to the measures and techniques by means of which the modulations of dynamics are achieved.

What we have called modulation is clearly a linear dynamic; but there is a lateral, or synchronic, dynamic as well. Therefore it is also during the process of revision that the 'mix' between inquiry and demonstration (which in the dissertation is the act of fulfilling degree requirements by means of rhetorical and structural *clichés*) may be adjusted. The book mix should be very rich indeed in inquiry, anaemic in demonstration. In the first reading after the post-dissertational fallow period its authenticity will reveal the quality of the former, while its counterfeiture will reveal the latter.

But not only this mix should be adjusted in the revision. There is also the word-idea ratio, as well as all the other aspects of synchronic structure. And the adjustment will be not for probity alone, but also for unity, for responsibility, and for style. Careful, unrelenting control over synchronic mix will produce a taut and pertinent continuum in the discourse – a continuum which, vital with diachronic modulations, will go far toward achieving a good book.

REVISION FOR RESPONSIBILITY

The revision of the work for responsibility is to move it fully from inquisition – in which the subject matter is tortured to death, its vitals strewn among inimical forms, inept techniques, and babbling footnotes – to inquiry which constitutes itself through words complete in all forms, fibres, and functions. The procreative task of the writer in his revision is to sire the work in words, carefully endowing it with germs of wholeness, fullness, and geneticity so that layer by layer, process by process, structure by structure, it becomes an organism.

The writer may well bear in mind during his re-reading the remarkable extent to which the serious book of nonfiction resembles the novel. That novel whose scene is not built to functional adequacy, whose characters are automatons, and whose acts are without credibility is a novel which lacks responsibility in the sense in which we have been using the term. The novelist must create a whole organism out of that organism's own parts. The world of the novel is thus constituted in believability. The same holds true of the scholarly work. It makes no difference that the one work deals with an imagined drama of the interactions of invented humans and the other with descriptions of or inventions about existential man or the real or hypothetical world. The obligation to create full-dimensional believability is as incumbent upon the writer of nonfiction as it is upon the writer of novels.

The inclusion of encyclopaedic detail does not achieve freestandingness in the scholarly book any more than it does in the novel. Indeed, as even the most patient reader knows, massive detail is tiresome and confusing; it smothers the work, makes it diffuse, and defeats the objective. Detail must be chosen with a clear sense of its significance *to the constitution of a whole and elegant organism*. Wholeness does not mean exhaustiveness; exhaustiveness yields exhaustion. It is for this reason that publishers reject a groaning weight of absolute documentation, abject demonstration, and utter datafication.

Thus the process of revision provides the prolix writer with the opportunity to carve away at the grossness of his work and the anaemic writer to add to his – both with the purpose of portraying *in line* tissues, processes, and structures. A responsible work is like a responsible bridge – a function of all the fibres and tensions it requires to exist as bridge. Decorations are not only baroque: they may jeopardize the possibility that the work will endure.

REVISION FOR UNITY

Presumably a successful dissertation has achieved that minimal unity of demonstra-

39

tion which broods like an ungainly but all-powerful tyrant over the good data, good thought, and good intentions it has usurped. At the same time it has achieved an acceptable degree of focus, which doubtless substitutes for genuine fixity. With these two pseudo-unities the dissertation may be submitted, and the degree secured.

But we know that the object of unity is to achieve a *genetic* unity in all strata of the work. Genetic unity is unity of thesis, unity of inquiry through the unities of probity and responsibility. These all add up to a *wholeness* of the work such that it becomes a fulfilled and fulfilling phenomenon energized with its inherent system of energies.

The achievement of wholeness results from the ever-growing mastery of the writer over his work. He succeeds in moulding together all aspects and faces so that they cohere and have plasticity, so that the work takes its natural, inevitable, and therefore most elegant form.

There is much more that ought to be said about revision and yet so little that can be said. I shall not even begin to speak of style, leaving that to the writer and to his external superego, his editor. I turn, instead, to the act of publishing.

PUBLICATION

A book is a verbal creation giving a perspective on man and the world. It is also a contribution to the sum of values, views, and attitudes which comprise the nature of man and his age, and shape his view of the cosmos. The greatest books establish perspectives that win belief and thus endure for generations, for centuries, or even for millennia. All this is in the nature of the book. But not until it is published. Publication is the natural end of the book; but it is not the natural end of the dissertation. The natural end of the dissertation is reached when the committee accepts it and the degree is granted. The dissertation is not a fact in the world of facts, but only a fact of the author's education. The publisher is more aware of this than most academicians, who, having directed their students in writing dissertations, advise them to submit these works to publishers; so it is that many publishers categorically decline to consider dissertations.

But the establishment of fact is a social prerogative. And so it follows that validation and objectification of the literary work is usually placed in the hands of the publisher whom the economics of success have confirmed as society's executor of its literary powers. Publishing is therefore to be seen as a normative activity which operates to define and maintain ideas, forms, and standards of discourse. The implications of this fact are enormous indeed, for in these terms publishing becomes on the one hand a dynamic of communications stability, and on the other an institutionalized inhibition upon the erratic and chaotic development of literary forms.

The normative characteristics of publishing do not result from a capricious

40

coalition of editors, however. Publishing persists by virtue of a kind of social contract among publishers, writers, and readers. Further, changes in the forms of communication (as opposed to the various *means* of communication, which change rapidly) tend to be slow. But it would be a disservice to the understanding of publishing if one were to permit the matter to stand at this, for it is clear that publishing is both positive and innovative – positive in the sense that it tends in the long run to be subject to historical changes, operating in accordance with the interests and practices of the day; and innovative in the sense that it often undertakes to incorporate in its processes a wide range of textual and structural mutations. It is clear, however, that such innovation is more likely to be found in the forms of fiction, verse, and interpretive nonfiction than in the scholarly book as we know it.

Only the most ardent determinist sees publishing solely as a process which inevitably expresses impersonal social forces. The more experienced observers recognize that it is infinitely personal as well, that individuals have profoundly and significantly shaped book publishing – notably, in trade publishing, Alfred A. Knopf, and possibly Horace Liveright as well. To name a similarly important person in university publishing – one who by his personality and taste helped shape an industry – is not possible, owing to the existence of the factor of university control which tends to minimize the more individualistic aspects of the publisher's role and to collectivize the interpretation of the functions of publishing, the character of the list, and the nature of the scholarship which goes to create that list.

The publisher as agent of society in publishing a book causes the latter to define its time not only for its author's day, but for the future as well. The publisher is thus the agent of history, and the author's book the projection of the author into the trajectory of history. It is as an effective delineator of the shape of his day and as an arbiter of history that the publisher completes the work of the author.

The publisher as the agent of these events is thus placed in a position of considerable power, and his obligations are accordingly very great. The best publishers are therefore those who are dedicated, through personal faith, to the most creative social ends – the university publisher generally to long-term ends, the commercial publisher generally, though by no means exclusively, to those more immediate ones in which he is a specialist, the satisfaction of which requires strategic contemporaneity of book and immediacy of sale.

But if the publisher is not merely a slave to the historical process it does not follow that he is without a sense of the sociality of his actions and of his responsibility for them. There are many significant evidences of the publisher's response in this respect, though we shall here mention but one, an evidence so basic to the publishing presence, however, as necessarily to become involved in any discussion of the nature of publishing. I am thinking of the dedication of a publishing house to the development

41

in depth of one or several specific disciplines or arts. In this respect one instantly thinks of specific examples: of Wesleyan University Press's dedication to new poets; of the role a house like New Directions has played in the development of new criticism; of Northwestern University Press's services in helping establish phenomenology as a vigorous philosophical movement in the United States. Thus the publisher may serve history by virtue of the fact that he can direct the present rather than merely rest content with reinforcing its values and practices.

But whether development- or service-oriented, publishing is definitive, adding by means of its strong strokes to the sharp delineation of the form and feature of its time. When the author submits his work to the publisher he enters into the historical process in a way that is more direct, immediate, and (save perhaps for producing children) more personal and irrevocable than all the other actions of his life. He has good reason therefore subsequently to have anxieties more compelling than those of mere waiting. He knows that now he must be prepared to go into history and to present himself at his best. His work is about to be judged for its probity, unity, and responsibility; its graces and its elegance; and its potentiality as a charge of energy induced into the accrued force of his epoch.

If the prospect of entering history is overwhelming – or unrealistic – and the possibility of contributing to the more or less ephemeral dialogue of one's day seems more probable, even so the publisher as an agent of society must legitimize the work, promising through the authority of his imprint that the work at least conforms to the nature of a book and deserves to be published. For the book for the day is no less a book than the book for the ages – it is only mortal rather than immortal. Its mortality is inherent in its thesis, the measure of its probity, its contemporaneity, and its restricted commitment to history and to universality.

No matter whether the work is to endure or soon to vanish, publication is the instrument of the processes of history, not only in creating the public record and content of a literary and intellectual history, but also in selecting and building those literary events which are to be the history of the epoch. No mere agent of tradition, then, but its generator, the publisher bears a final and awesome relationship to the writer's book.

Given the social and historical nature of the act of publishing, it is not surprising that the process of bringing the book into being should be as normative as the original act of selection. Thus both in the editing and in the designing of the book, the canons of the best language and the best appearance are invoked to make the book a product of its day. In most American publishing houses two different kinds of editors are ordinarily involved in the process of turning the author's work into a printed book. The one with whom the writer initially engages, the acquisitions or sponsoring editor, makes the first expression of interest; if he likes the work and wishes it to be published, he presents it to the head of the house with his recommen-dation. Prior to this, of course, he both reads the work himself and sends it to special-ist readers for criticism. If in his judgement their opinions warrant proceeding, he urges publication.

It is this editor who will recommend to the author those major revisions he and his readers deem necessary or desirable. Often this occurs prior to the offering of a contract, although not always. The work is, of course, the author's, and the decision to accept or reject the recommended changes is his as well. But the money is the publisher's, and if the writer is reluctant to make the suggested changes, the publisher may not be willing to proceed with the negotiations and may not offer a contract. If the publisher has sufficient confidence in the work, however, he may decide to go along on the writer's terms.

After the questions of major revision have been adjudicated, the manuscript is placed in the hands of the manuscript editor, with whom the writer may expect a prolonged relationship of considerable intimacy – an intimacy both professional and personal, both intellectual and emotional. This relationship is an important one, falling only slightly behind that of the writer's relationship with his family and his analyst (if any). The editor reads the work more carefully and (if this is not too great a paradox to contemplate) with greater *detached empathy* than either the author's friends or his enemies subsequently will. The editor learns the work habits of the writer's mind, its strengths and its shortcomings, those shortcuts it is likely to seek and the turgid prolixities it may sometimes like to effect when it knows but won't admit it is not going any place. The manuscript editor evaluates and exploits the writer's talents, to the end of helping him to mobilize *all* his resources so that he can produce the very best book of which he is capable. If American published scho-larship is on the whole and in certain conspicuous respects better than much Euro-pean and British scholarship, this is owing largely to the creative co-operation of the relatively small corps of devoted manuscript editors.

And yet, *mirabile dictu*, the good manuscript editor achieves so much (much more than the author's analyst in all probability, by the way) without stridency. That this is so is sometimes a monument to human endurance with dignity, for unfortunately some authors are insolent without cause, arrogant with no justifica-tion, proud of their misuse of the English language, and intemperate in their satisfaction with their own abilities. Fortunately, such traits are frequently visible from afar and, barring the major work of genius, small attention need be paid to the antics – which often are excessive in direct ratio to the mediocrity of the work. A good manuscript editor, being more long-suffering than the writer of this article, would very likely not have written the above. I do it gratuitously on that editor's behalf. Some bold soul must set the record straight!

But the time comes when both author's and editor's options are limited. The work is brought into final form. Now the book is neither the author's nor the publisher's, it becomes its own, its freestandingness finally achieved. It is now sent to the designer.

The design of the book, too, is normative, in the sense that it reflects the designer's idea of how a book of the kind ought to look. At the same time, however, it is also positive in that it reflects the day's prevailing aesthetics of design, and, indeed, the *weltgefühl* of its period. Design is more subject to rapid change than editorial practices, as may be seen by comparing the two features in books from the 1920s, for example, with those of today. A further consideration must be borne in mind as well, namely, that design is an expressive dimension, not only of the taste of the age but also of the content of the book. Design thus rounds out the act of pre-emption which the epoch asserts upon its books – as it does indeed upon all its other productions as well, and the designer quite as clearly and as decisively as the acquisitions and manuscript editors executes the dictates of society and makes a contribution to history. The cut of the typeface (whether linear or cursive, with or without serifs), the style of designing a page (open or tight, with or without wide margins), the setting of the lines to execute this design, the finish and the colour of the paper – all these variables express the prevailing taste. Design at its best also expresses the particularity of the book, the designer using both the visual properties of the type and the degree of interlinear and intercharacter space to express such aspects of the text as its conformity or its freedom, its gravity or its superficiality, its propriety or its irreverence.

Yet if I portray the publisher only as an agent of abstract social forces I am being a simple-minded determinist. Culture, society, and history all move upon multiple feet, like a horrendous and mutated millipede whose countless feet are the untold humans who constitute it. The publisher works with the particular books of particular authors, and the good publisher never forgets the human rootedness of the books he publishes. He knows that he produces self-sustaining surrogates for the author, and that no matter how much the book may become divorced from the man – even though the author should be or through time should become anonymous – yet the publisher knows it is a particular voice that speaks. He does not forget, therefore, that the ultimate term constituting the personal equation in publishing is the discrete work of a particular author. Though he be inexorably acting out the grand designs of social forces, the good publisher never subordinates his author to considerations of a vast and impersonal social design. He realizes that in the final analysis the act of publishing is the act of publishing a man, whose work is his personal and intellectual odyssey. Although on publication of the work the publisher causes it to be divorced from the author, as mother is divorced at birth from child, yet does he know that the author has still to enjoy the pride of creation that comes from seeing the work take its place in the dynamic of its discipline and its day.

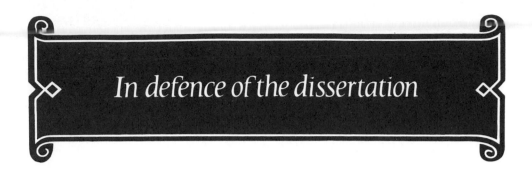

In defence of the dissertation

WILLIAM W. SAVAGE, JR

If the recent assaults made upon the dissertation in the pages of this journal are an indication of a growing trend in university press publishing, they are equally indicative of an editorial perspective that is, like the pedantry it deplores, unfortunately narrow and ultimately detrimental to the symbiotic relationship between the press and the academic community. The dissertation and the circumstances from which it arises should be – must be – viewed in as broad a context as possible for the benefit of all concerned.

To condemn is a simple matter, and to condemn the dissertation is the simplest of all. From the editor's standpoint, the dissertation is seldom if ever ideal, either in conception or execution. Often it is downright damnable. Robert Plant Armstrong has ably summarized the prevailing criticisms, and there is no need to pursue them here. What should be of concern, however, is the fact that these criticisms too often go beyond the dissertation and deal directly with its author, as though he (or if he is a mindless dupe, his director) must be held responsible for inflicting a boorish exercise on the already overburdened editor. Attitudes of this kind merely compound everyone's problems.

The point, quite simply, is this: editors do not write dissertations, and graduate students do not make books. The two endeavours are not mutually exclusive, but their coalescence is, to say the very least, infrequent. The result is misunderstanding, attended by disillusionment, frustration, and anger. Editors want one thing, but writers of dissertations produce another, and when the work is submitted, conflict to a greater or lesser extent is inevitable. The most farsighted of the antagonists blame the 'system' – editors, the system that spawns dissertations; writers, the system that spawns editors – and nowhere does there seem to be common ground.

What editors and dissertation writers fail to perceive is that they function in similar circumstances and that their disagreements result from minor differences between their respective 'systems.' In this connection, editors might do well to consider the intellectual life of the graduate student. Depending upon the individual and the particular university he attends, that life may be only vaguely linked to the classroom or the whims of a dissertation director. Books are the graduate student's stock in trade, and he must read widely – not, perhaps, for the sake of his dissertation, but to satisfy his intellectual curiosity and to overcome the more immediate obstacles of written and oral examinations. If he is thinking ahead, he reads incisively, observing prose style in its component aspects and filing away information for use later. He may imagine his own work in print, but that is incidental to his goal. He is immersed in the printed page, absorbing what the press and its editor have put there and, more importantly perhaps, *how* they have put it. Seminars reinforce the latter perception: notes are placed at the foot of the page, and sometimes they explain things, and sometimes they are long. A bibliography follows the text. These are prepared according to a certain style. Turabian offers a style. Books are to be imitated.

It is hardly surprising, then, that the student equates dissertations with books. Whatever their differences, they *look* alike. Moreover, respected scholars say they *are* alike. To Jacques Barzun, they are the same. To Louis Gottschalk, their differences are imperceptible. An editor will correct that impression a few years later, or try to, but for the time being it is set firmly in the student's mind. And if the student follows the format he sees, does he not adopt the language he reads? The problems grow.

Consider now the editor, also immersed in books. Examine his work. Knowingly or not, he has contributed at every turn to the evils of the dissertation. A substantial part of his press's backlist consists of revised dissertations, wherein Turabian bows to *A Manual of Style*. Some are better than others. A few were published because of their sales potential. Others were subsidized by foundations and institutions. Some should never have been published at all. Each one, good, bad, or indifferent, is both an advertisement for the press and an offering for the advancement of scholarship. The new PH.D.'s decision to submit the dissertation that now occupies the editor's desk was prompted by one or more of those books, perhaps by the tome his mentor wrote – the one still in its first printing after twenty years. Eventually the realization must come that what you publish is what you get, but nevertheless, the editor blames the dissertation's author for his daily chore. He may urge acceptance of the dissertation, for any of several reasons and regardless of its defects, and if he does, he perpetuates that which he finds deplorable.

Clearly the editor and graduate student can find common, if not felicitous, ground. The diligence of one can create examples to prevent the future errors of the other. Both, however, should realize that they expect too much from the dissertation. They have forgotten what it was designed to be, and they ignore what it is. Like any piece of writing, it is practice for the next, and the fact that the next may never come is wholly irrelevant. The German dissertation, moreover, was structured for oral defence, not publication, and a century of academic mutation has not succeeded in altering that structure, despite the new purposes to which the American version has been put. If the student considers his dissertation a book, he is surely no more unreasonable than the editor who expects it to be one.

Whatever the solution to the dissertation dilemma may be, it does not lie in the prospect of revolutionary change in the graduate programs of American universities. The PH.D. octopus that William James described is growing still and shows no signs of pulling in its tentacles. Thus the dissertation, like other facts of life, will remain with us. If anything changes, it will have to be the way in which university presses deal with it. And decisions in that regard should not be made in the heat of unreasoning criticism, unless presses are fully prepared to abandon the academic community and the support it provides. With all its attendant flaws, the dissertation is more satisfactory than most starting points for bookmaking, and that, too, is a fact of life.

Avoiding the warmed-over dissertation

WILLIAM C. DOWLING

As someone who has been involved for several years now in the lonely process of trying to rewrite his doctoral dissertation as a book, I've been following with interest the series of essays *Scholarly Publishing* has recently devoted to the subject—with considerable interest, and even (I confess) with some trepidation: I'd necessarily formed my own conclusions some time ago, and wasn't anxious to have them proved wrong. But the essays have all stressed a point from which a beginning scholar can only derive comfort: 'The book ... is a humane work which the writer intends to be taken seriously' (Robert Plant Armstrong); 'A scholarly work of analysis or criticism should impart to the reader the writer's conviction that his subject is worth writing about and worth reading about' (Francess Halpenny).

The path a junior scholar travels in reaching this same conclusion, however, is not so comfortable, and as I was reading I kept remembering my own anxieties three years ago, when I hadn't yet begun to rewrite. The concerns of a young PH.D. are not at that moment Olympian, and his question, as he sits at his desk with two bound copies of his dissertation beside him, is distressingly practical: 'Very well, but *how*?' I'm not sure I know the answer to that question yet, but it's one that has concerned me closely for some time.

When I began to think about writing a book, a curious thing happened: I found myself turning over the pages of scholarly works I'd known for years, and some which I'd never have opened otherwise, with a new and critical eye – looking for models. And here the practical worries began: the classics, which were of course the works to emulate, were almost always written by seasoned scholars in their intellectual prime; they were inspiring, but at the moment impossible as models.

48

But then, sitting in great profusion on the shelves of my local bookstore, were all the others: books which were not books at all but warmed-over dissertations – precisely the kind of thing one is determined not to write.

The warmed-over dissertation will some day, I hope, be regarded as an embarrassing episode in the history of scholarly publishing, recalling the unwary exuberance of university presses in the sixties. But the young PH.D., determined to make his first book a real contribution to his field, is unlikely to take comfort in any long-term historical perspective, for his immediate concern is to avoid the genre altogether. His question, once again, is severely practical: what distinguishes the warmed-over dissertation from the genuine scholarly book which happens to have its origin in research undertaken for a dissertation?

My bookstore research, casual as it was, seemed to suggest at least one useful distinction: the genuine book is an elaboration of a single significant idea, and the warmed-over dissertation isn't. To borrow Robert Plant Armstrong's phrase, the warmed-over dissertation is a 'non-thesis book,' and its author, working without a strong central conception, cannot hope to solve his problems with revision.

There are a number of easily observed features, I found, which distinguish the thesis book from the non-thesis one. In my own field (literary criticism), the warmed-over dissertation is almost certain to have a fancy non-descriptive main title (*The Naked Dreamer: A Study of James Joyce*) and a battery of epigraphs at the beginning of each new chapter; its text will consist of a plodding succession of commentary and quotes, quotes and commentary. The non-introduction to a non-thesis book provides either a perfunctory review-of-scholarship-on-the-subject or an incoherent bill of fare ('While my main concern is with x, I have attempted to deal also with y, and have glanced briefly at z'). Here are some phrases gleaned from one such introduction:

> *Although I do not actually conclude that ...*
> *I am basically more concerned with ...*
> *My own interest is in ... though I also deal with ....*
> *But even though I will generalize in this area, I will not devote myself to ...*
> *In contrast to most critics of ——, I argue that ...*
> *The heart of my interest is in ...*
> *Because of this emphasis I can refer only fleetingly if at all to ...*

The dilemma of the author without an argument is implicit in these phrases, and they provide a perfect illustration of what the young scholar contemplating his first book wishes to avoid. To me, this seemed to suggest an obvious starting point for a systematic approach to rewriting: since the warmed-over dissertation is a monograph in belated search of an idea, the process should probably begin with the question, 'Do I really have an idea?'

Once I brought myself to the point of asking this question, I remember, it became less dismaying than it sounds: there surely couldn't be anything very ignoble in coming to the honest conclusion that I hadn't said anything immensely significant in the dissertation, and turning my energies to writing separate essays on the two or three more important points I'd developed. But after several long evenings in my office, rereading the dissertation and drinking coffee and trying to be as objective as possible, I decided that I'd been lucky – somewhere in there, hidden in a tangle of notes and commentary and digressions, was a reasonably promising main idea.

At this point came another painful moment of self-examination: was that main idea important enough to justify a full-length study? If it wasn't, I decided, my best option was the same as before: I'd have material for a major article but not for a book, and my effort had best go into writing a polished and soundly developed essay. After a few more nights of coffee and solitude, though, it did seem as though the idea might be worth pursuing for two or three hundred pages, and I began thinking about the next step.

The next step, which surprised me when I finally got to it, was to write the introduction. Since the introduction to every non-thesis book I looked at gave the impression of being an afterthought, a last-ditch attempt to justify a work with no real argument, it seemed clear that the author of a book with an important point to make should use his introduction to present this main idea clearly and compellingly, and to awaken his reader's interest in the detailed discussion to follow. The introduction to a thesis book, it seemed to me, should stand almost as an essay in itself, except that it would be full of points which begged for further elaboration.

That, at any rate, was the theory. When I actually sat down to write, I admit that I found the whole prospect somewhat intimidating – the first thirty pages of my dissertation were a hopeless example of the muddled non-introduction, and I soon realized that I'd embarked on a new and fairly demanding project. But in the next month or so, as my introduction took shape, I became more and more convinced that I'd chosen the right course.

The best reason for writing the introduction first, I discovered, was eminently practical: it compels you to refine your argument at the beginning of revision, when it's most essential to do so. Since you've already done a dissertation on your subject, there's little danger of straying into unsupported generalization, and the introduction becomes a place where you can develop the broader implications of your main concept at the same time as you introduce it.

The final step, of course, is to rewrite everything else. Once again, my experience has confirmed the practical wisdom of beginning with the introduction. If the introduction is an honest and competent piece of work, the benefits begin to appear immediately: with a firm sense of direction, you have little trouble realigning your original insights with your major point, getting rid of smothering documentation and digressive or irrelevant material, and (one hopes) gracefully subordinating the particular to the general. When the rewriting is finished, there is some reason to hope that it is the rough draft not of a warmed-over dissertation but of a book.

A rough draft is only that, of course, and there are still visions and revisions (about five revisions) to come, and even then there's no guarantee that the manuscript is publishable, or that any publisher will take it. But the experience of trying to write a genuinely thoughtful and learned work, it seems to me, is indispensable for anyone seriously committed to scholarship, and carries its own reward. That was once the rationale behind the doctoral dissertation, and even now, when the dissertation has become an empty ritual, it is a sound one.

One final observation: Henri Peyre suggests that 'the solution to the widespread unease now experienced by publishers, readers, graduate schools, and young scholars probably lies in ... the abandonment of the dissertation for all young doctors at the end of their training,' Robert Plant Armstrong (to the emphatic contrary) that 'there is every reason why, in this day of PH.D. overproduction, the requirement to write a dissertation should be dropped and the requirement to write a book substituted.'

Armstrong's solution is surely the correct one: if a new-model car shows a high incidence of brake failure, we do not conclude that the manufacturer should stop putting brakes into his automobiles, but that he should put in better ones. Armstrong is implicitly arguing, it seems to me, for a total reform of graduate education, one which would reinstate the PH.D. as a symbol of scholarly and intellectual competence, and would attract to the academic profession only the people who are fitted for it by talent and commitment. This is the only answer: the widespread unease Professor Peyre describes is real, but it is mostly the dissatisfaction of people who don't know why they're doing what they're doing, and who are unhappily convinced that it is too late to change.

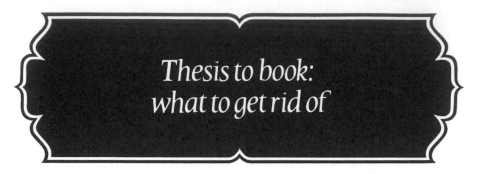

Thesis to book: what to get rid of

OLIVE HOLMES

PART I

The art of communication is one of the arts of survival for the scholar. If he takes seriously the command to 'publish or perish,' writing well becomes a matter of life and death. He is not, therefore, in a mood of confident relaxation when he approaches that blank page, and his anxiety may be responsible for some of the common defects of academic writing.

The first book manuscript prepared by the beginning academic writer is very often his PH.D. thesis, which he submits to a publisher either as it stands or following substantial revision. In making the suggestions that follow I am not recommending this practice nor am I against it. I am aware that some writers of PH. D. theses are quite content to have their work remain in that category and have no great desire to publish a book. I am also aware that some theses are so well written that they do not need much further editing to become publishable. Nor do I equate a thesis with poor writing and a book with good writing, or suggest that one is necessarily inferior to the other. The point is that a thesis and a book are different. If the scholar understands this difference, he is more apt to wind up with a publishable manuscript.

A thesis is written to display knowledge, to persuade, and to impress. It is written for a specific reward – a degree, and for a specific audience – a committee of specialists. It is a demonstration of the writer's ability to handle research as well as a report on a particular subject, and is involved with method as well as content. Since it is a test of a certain kind of expertise, it falls into the category of examination with all the emphasis on how well the student performs. Content is more important than communication, the author (and his ability) more important than either.

The purpose of a book is quite different. A book is primarily a communication, whether it is about the control of aphids or T'ang sculpture, the Dead Sea Scrolls or the Pentagon Papers. A book in some cases is indeed a performance but it exists apart from its author as a child exists apart from its parents. The reader is not primarily interested in the author but in the book.

A book does not talk to itself but discloses something to someone. The author of a book concentrates on getting his ideas across rather than making an impression. In so doing, he shifts his attention from himself to the work at hand. He sets aside his personal goals and reaches out to make his ideas clear to others. Paradoxically, he will be more objective while putting more of himself into his work. Since much of good writing comes out of the ends of the fingers, the author now has to use more of his subconscious mind, which, in his preoccupation with rational thinking, he may have ignored. He is, in effect, now adding art to scholarship in order to communicate fully. Many scholars are culture-bound in the sense that their concentration on the purely intellectual has caused them to denigrate feeling. Even a feeling for words sometimes seems to them to be faintly orgiastic.

A book, then, is not a warmed-over or patched-up thesis. The evolution from one to the other demands a whole new approach, a different way of looking at the material, of envisioning the reader, and even a new motivation. As he writes a thesis, an author is still a student; when he tries to turn it into a book, he is a writer, and a writer has obligations to his reader. The reader is a man to be reckoned with, not as judge and jury, but as a person to be informed, to be enlightened, even to be rescued, for as E.B. White, relaying the words of his teacher, has written: 'Will [Strunk] felt that the reader was in serious trouble most of the time, a man floundering in a swamp, and that it was the duty of anyone attempting to write English to drain this swamp quickly and get this man up on dry ground, or at least throw him a rope.'[1] The thesis writer is not concerned about throwing a rope to his doctoral committee. He is hoping they will fling one to him. But as a book author, his attitude has to change to one of tender consideration for the man floundering in the swamp. If the author can make this mental shift, he is on his way to becoming the writer of a book. He might even find that his efforts lead him into a maturing and invigorating experience.

THE TRUMPETER EFFECT

The first step in the transformation of a thesis into a book is to get rid of the signs of a thesis. This is essentially a negative process, but it has to come first.

The most common of these signs is the 'trumpeter effect' or 'bulletin-board announcement.' So accustomed is the thesis writer to the blackboard background that he tends to interrupt himself by posting notices. He never quite manages to live in the present of his work – only in its past and the future. There is consequently a lot of pointing out, reminding, and referring – signposts which an intelligent reader resents. For example:

> *This chapter will deal with the first period of the Cordovan Caliphate. The second period will be dealt with in the following chapter ...*

> *In a later section of this chapter further information will be presented to elaborate on the question of the value of the click beetle as predator ...*

It is also unnecessary to tell the captive reader what he has just read. Presumably he is not spot-checking the book. The author hopes and should assume that every word will be read, even though this is probably optimistic. (A scholarly writer might as well be resigned to the fact that every word of his book may not and probably will not be read, particularly if it has a good index – that boon to the busy academic.) In any event, there is no need to remind the reader what the last chapter was about.

> *The August seventh agenda of the Steering Committee of the Society for the Suppression of Pornographic Literature has already been analyzed in my last chapter.*

> *Most of the relevant changes in the relations between the third assistant secretary and the leader of the Youth Caucus have been illustrated in a discussion of other issues in our first two chapters. See also Appendix Yc.*

Sometimes an author not only backtracks but announces that there is no need to. When he says: 'There should be no need to recapitulate the factors' which led up to the outbreak of the Civil War or the settlement of the railroad strike or which entered into his decision to turn his thesis into a book – the reader is tempted to reply: 'Then don't!' The trouble with all this forewarning and recapitulating is that it makes the reader feel like a spectator seated near the centre line at a tennis match or like a guest speaker forced to sit through a business meeting of the Women's Auxiliary of the Society for the Preservation of the Cyrus P. Titherington Homestead before he is permitted to begin his address. The announcements of meeting times and places, of postponements, acknowledgements, and arrangements are not in the realm of either speechmaking or literature and must simply be got through. The mind, in fact, wanders. That may be exciting at a tennis match, or endurable for the members at a business meeting, but is ruinous for a book. If the reader's mind wanders, the author may never get it back again.

One reason for this tendency to seesaw between past and future is that most writers of theses are also teachers or, as students, have been long exposed to teaching techniques including advance warning and repetition. The teacher often points out what the next lesson is going to be, and reviews the last one. He may do so to remind the absent-minded student that there are lesson assignments and ignorance of them is no excuse; but the habit becomes a part of a teacher's equipment and creeps into his writing, even for his peers. Repetition is a deliberate technique in the classroom, but less desirable in books. Readers are not smarter and not necessarily more wide awake than students, but they do have the advantage of having all the words in one place where they can look forward or back at will. A news commentator may feel he needs to recap the top story for the benefit of latecomers in his audience. But this is not one of the author's worries. (He has many others to make up for it.) The audience of one reader has been there all the time.

When an author puts up signposts, he is talking down. He is saying to the reader, in effect: 'You can't really do this on your own. You need a guided tour. Let me take you by the hand.' But the most compelling reason for cutting out all these announcements is that they are a dead giveaway that the author's work is still in thesis form. His outline is showing through.

The outline, which helped him to organize his thoughts, should now disappear. The artist conceals his art. The painter does not exhibit his pre-liminary sketches (unless he is a Picasso). The first draft of the Declaration of Independence, on exhibit in the Library of Congress, is a reminder of the universal human tendency to stumble in and out of sentences. Since there are few Picassos or Jeffersons among us, it would seem best to delete those first tentative efforts and forget them. An outline is only a thinking aid, not an end.

The writer should now seek to draw attention not to himself and to his worthiness as a degree candidate but to his subject. One of the most effective and quickest ways to achieve this step forward is to search the manuscript for moments when, in the words of Emerson, he 'postpones or remembers,' and eliminate them. Living in the present, highly recommended for everyone by Emerson, is a particular virtue in a writer.

THE APOLOGETIC OPENING

Closely related to the trumpeter effect is the apologetic opening. It is a limp cousin to the hyperactive forewarning and summing up. There is an excruciating false modesty about the preface that plunges immediately into an explanation of what the author has *not* done, giving lengthy reasons. There is also a great misunderstanding of the reader's reactions. First impressions are important. If the author sidles up to his subject and then starts moving crabwise over a host of negative statements, it is a patient reader indeed who will bother to go further. The reaction is, if the author has not done all this, what in the world did he do?

> *Although I do not feel that I have covered the ground that should have been covered, because of the paucity of sources, an attempt has been made, however, to bring out certain aspects of the subject which have seemingly, although not entirely, some foundation. Consequently, there are large areas which have not been touched upon. I must also point out that there are some doubts about the authenticity of the Granville Documents and I tend to share the conclusions of some authors who believe that they are entirely suspect. I was also not able to spend all the time I would have liked to in the family archives of Englebert, Lord Pricklypear, for reasons which I shall not go into here.*

And so on, and on. At the end of this chronicle of non-accomplishment and self-doubt, one wonders what can possibly be contained in the six to eight hundred pages that follow. One is not inclined to try to find out.

It does not seem possible that the above example could be made more apologetic but some authors transcend it by stating that they are not going to be apologetic – which has the peculiar effect of a crab scuttling diagonally backwards:

> *Instead of offering a long apology for choosing this topic, I should like at*
> *the outset to delimit the subject of this book ... I shall not predict the future*
> *nor shall I talk about the crucial problem of the relationship between ...*
> *I have to ignore the important question ...*

This is a kind of trumpeter effect in reverse as well as an apologetic substitute for an apology, all of which adds up to a most effective device to 'delimit' the reader's interest.

The necessity to explain oneself is, of course, a thesis hangover, a piece of self-consciousness, which should be discarded. The nonprofessional reader cheerfully assumes that if the author is writing a book, he probably has some good reasons for it, not the least of which is that he has something to say. It is not really necessary to go into the whys and wherefores too deeply, unless these are special or peculiar. If someone writes a book on living in a commune in the South African bush, the reader might perhaps be interested in how he happened on the topic. But normally the reader will expect him simply to go ahead and tell whatever story he has to tell.

Is the scholarly book different in this matter? No. The research for it has usually, although not always, been carried out in libraries, and an explanation may sometimes be required of how the facts were obtained. Otherwise one may be guilty of the vice of the unsupported statement – true. But these are matters best confined to the backmatter. A note at the head of the bibliography can be useful when the author feels compelled to explain.

I've never known a scholar yet who was not conscious of some deficiencies when writing a book, but an introduction is not the place to dwell upon them. One should not cease being genuinely modest and aware of how much remains to be done, but it is better to look on the bright side at what has been accomplished in relation to this book, and give oneself, and the reader, a break. Life is short, art and scholarship are long. It's the finished product that matters in both of the latter, not the sketches and skirmishes. When the product is good, there is no need to apologize for it. If it is not, no amount of apology will make it any better. A book stands on its own.

Some theses give the impression of having been written in a crowded study with a number of the author's colleagues peeking over his shoulder making comments. The author, unfortunately, becomes self-conscious in the presence of so many of his peers or of those who have gone before him. It is a bit like having ancestors glaring down from the portraits on the walls.

The nature of scholarship is to build on the work of others, and rightly so, and the work of others must be acknowledged. Again it is not a question of either/or but of how much. A thesis, far more than a book, will normally mention the work of others, either to agree or to disagree with them. Sometimes this kind of thing gets into internecine academic feuds with which the general reader has no patience. The specialist may be interested to know that La Flamme's theories, first expounded in 1899, were superseded by Von Humpack's in 1905, and that nothing of any great value had been done in this area of research until the author himself overturned both La Flamme and Von Humpack by his brilliant diagnosis of the nature of their fallacies and a complete exposure of their mistakes. But to most potential readers this is footnote information, not the main thrust of the work, a sideshow that sometimes can be pretty interesting but most of the time is a great bore.

I am not suggesting that the contributions of others be ignored, only that they be put in their proper place with a proper emphasis. They can be interruptive, and when pushed to an extreme they throw the book off balance into a discussion of other people's work. A book crowded with the ghosts of the author's scholarly ancestors creaks like a haunted house.

In his delightful spoof, *The Pooh Perplex*, Frederick C. Crews parodies such academic sparring in a chapter entitled 'Paradoxical Persona: The Hierarchy of Heroism in Winnie-the-Pooh,' by a mythical Harvey C. Windrow.

> *It is, then, with a sense of my own temerity – if not indeed, of outright rashness – that I must assert that Ogle, Smythe, Bunker, and Wart have completely missed the point of Pooh. Valuable as their studies have been in establishing certain connections and parallels that other scholars might not have thought were worth pursuing, I cannot honestly say that we have learned anything significant from them. Neither Ogle, nor Smythe, nor Bunker, nor Wart asked himself the absolutely basic questions about Winnie-the-Pooh, and thus each of them necessarily failed*

to grasp the key to the book's entire meaning. I find myself in the embarrassing position of being the only possessor of this key, and I am writing this essay only to alter such an unbalanced situation as quickly as possible.[2]

The social scientists argue that their work is different from the historian's and literary critic's and this is partly true. They claim that they are more concerned with methodology than the historian, that because they are still working out approaches and systems, the mechanics of their research is an important subject. They are still, as I understand it, absorbed in their own technique. This need not mean, however, that the author should not try to get beyond a limitation (and this absorption in methodology is a limitation, as far as clarity and readability are concerned) to the happy land where technique is subordinate to communication.

THE WARM-UP PERIOD

The first four or five pages of a first draft are, more often than not, dispensable. Ask any author or editor where he looks first for cuts and he will probably answer that the beginning of a manuscript offers the greatest chance of compression. The reason is simple. We tend to go through a warm-up period, a time of flexing muscles, of sharpening pencils, of trying to put off the evil day, and of just getting into the material. Much of that preliminary skirmishing stays in a manuscript even unto the second and third drafts. It is hard to cut because it is sometimes hard to recognize one's own meanderings. But, once aware of our own habits and the normal human fear of exposure, we can overcome the tendency to go the long way around. In writing it is not the shortest way home.

Although there are as many ways of writing as there are writers, one highly recommended and widely used technique is to work in two distinct stages: 1 / the first draft, which is written with abandon – fully and freely and uncritically; 2 / the second draft, which is looked at by its author with a critical and analytical eye. Probably a few days, at least, should intervene between these two stages, time enough to let the author change gears.

It seems to me that there are certain advantages in this way of working. One is that the subconscious rises closer to the surface if given a longer period of time to do so, rids us of inhibitions, and does more of the work for us. Another is that early meanderings are more apparent and more easily overcome once an entire first draft is complete, because there is a sense of the whole and consequently a greater perspective. But I have known writers who polish each paragraph as they go along and who apparently work much better in shorter bursts. We can discover the method that suits each of us best only by experimenting.

If the two-stage plan is followed, during the second stage the author should be able to recognize how much stalling he is actually doing. We all tend to play around the edges, trying not to get our feet wet, when usually a dive into the deep part of the pool is more effective. Jacques Barzun calls this timidity 'the writer's insidious desire to put a cozy padded vest between his tender self and that vague, hostile roaming animal known as the audience.' His remedy is to 'convince yourself that you are working in clay not marble, on paper not eternal bronze: let that first sentence be as stupid as it wishes. No one will rush out and print it as it stands.'[3]

It has been said that a play must be established in the first thirty seconds. Although the techniques of the dramatist and the author of expository prose are different, there is much to be learned from the playwright – especially, in this context, his skill in getting started. He has, of course, visual means to help him: the set, the living people, the costumes and props. But he also uses speech, and the first words he chooses are of the utmost importance. At the next play you see, think how much information is given within the first few minutes. See how soon it is made clear what the play is all about. We need go no further than Shakespeare, as usual. *Romeo and Juliet* opens with:

> *Two households, both alike in dignity,*
> *In fair Verona, where we lay our scene,*
> *From ancient grudge break to new mutiny,*
> *Where civil blood makes civil hands unclean.*
> *From forth the fatal loins of these two foes*
> *A pair of star-cross'd lovers take their life.*

And Dylan Thomas began *Under Milk Wood* with his First Voice saying very softly: 'To begin at the beginning.'[4] There is the memorable first minute or so of *Our Town*, and, on a somewhat different level, the shock opening of the mystery in which a corpse falls out of the closet as soon as the curtain goes up. It is clear from the start what these plays are going to be about.

I am not advocating shock openings for a scholarly work. But a feel for this kind of thing will help an author discover how to cut a lengthy preamble down to a few well-chosen words that will give the reader some sense of what he is in for. Here is a good opening sentence for a scholarly work:

> *On May 4, 1919, students in Peking demonstrated in protest against the Chinese government's humiliating policy toward Japan. There resulted a series of strikes and associated events amounting to a social ferment and an intellectual revolution. This rising tide was soon dubbed by the students the May Fourth Movement.*[5]

The book is, not surprisingly, about the May Fourth Movement.

Erich Fromm began *The Sane Society* with: 'Nothing is more common than the idea that we, the people living in the Western world of the twentieth century, are eminently sane.' We discover almost immediately that Fromm is going to challenge this idea when the second paragraph opens: 'Can we be so sure that we are not deceiving ourselves?'[6]

David Riesman started *The Lonely Crowd* without beating around the bush:

> *This is a book about social character, and about the differences in social character between men of different regions, eras, and groups. It considers the ways in which different social character types, once they are formed at the knee of society, are then deployed in the work, play, politics, and child-rearing activities of society.*[7]

If you feel that you are skirting around a subject or leading up to it on a long, winding path, think about what you actually want to say with this book after all the tortured months or perhaps years of research. Can you still see the forest for the trees? Try to sum up your book in a few words. Impossible? Not really. But even if you do not succeed, the mere attempt may help to get closer to the real subject and come to grips with it. Readers will be grateful.

Search, too, for repetitions. They are particularly rampant during the process of getting started. Circular prose should wind up in the circular file. A warm-up period is necessary in writing, as in most other activities, so the meanderings get down on paper. The trouble is that sometimes they stay there. Warming up should not be allowed to occupy valuable space in the finished product.

1 / William Strunk, Jr., and E. B. White, *The Elements of Style*, 2nd ed (New York: Macmillan Company, 1972), p. xii

2 / Frederick C. Crews, *The Pooh Perplex: A Freshman Casebook* (New York: Dutton, 1963)

3 / Jacques Barzun, *On Writing, Editing, and Publishing* (Chicago: University of Chicago Press, 1971), pp. 8, 9

4 / Dylan Thomas, *Under Milk Wood: A Play for Voices* (New York: James Laughlin, 1954)

5 / Chow Tse-tsung, *The May Fourth Movement* (Cambridge, Mass.: Harvard University Press, 1960)

6 / Erich Fromm, *The Sane Society* (New York: Holt, Rinehart and Winston, Inc., 1955)

7 / David Riesman, *The Lonely Crowd: A Study of the Changing American Character* (New Haven: Yale University Press, 1950); paperback edition, Yale University Press, 1961

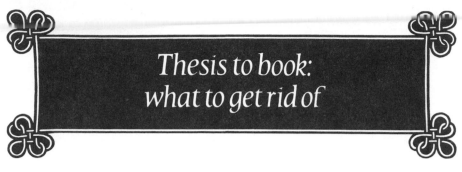

Thesis to book: what to get rid of

OLIVE HOLMES

PART II

LENGTH

The day of lengthy treatises of any sort may be passing. The luxury of spreading oneself in space or time simply does not fit in with modern technology. Verbosity is expensive. Books may necessarily become shorter and shorter except, of course, for best-sellers, which can still be allowed some width on the bookshelf because they pay their way. The time may come when the only fat books will be the wildly popular ones.

This trend would be sad if it were not true that shorter is often better. A long book is frequently long only because it has too many words. It is perhaps a commentary on present-day standards that we have to be driven to write with telling brevity not by the desire to communicate well but by the need to cut costs. Yet long before the age of soaring printing costs, the best writers whittled at their prose. Thoreau wrote in a letter to a friend: 'Don't suppose that you can tell it precisely the first dozen times you try, but at 'em again ... Not that the story need be long, but it will take a long time to make it short.'[1]

Cutting a manuscript is not simply a way of reducing length; it is also a way of strengthening communication. It is always hard to convince anyone that less is more, that the still small voice speaks louder, that fewer words are stronger, that a good thought needs no embellishment, and that one good sentence goes a long way. But there is a psychological reason for preferring brevity: 'By reducing the span of attention required we increase the force of the thought.'[2] Ideas come through more clearly if there are fewer of them in each sentence or paragraph. Sentences come through more clearly if there are fewer words in them, and one good word is worth two mediocre ones. With this standard in mind, pruning becomes a positive process, not merely cutting down or out, casting away, or bulldozing, but careful surgery that results in health, strength, and vitality.

There are two major ways of cutting a manuscript: one is by searching for repetitions and unneeded quotations and cutting out whole hunks; the other is to do what is known as 'inner cutting,' that is, eliminating paragraphs, sentences, and words. Strunk delivered the classic statement about pruning prose:

> *Vigorous writing is concise. A sentence should contain no unnecessary words, a paragraph no unnecessary sentences, for the same reason that a drawing should have no unnecessary lines and a machine no unnecessary parts. This requires not that the writer make all his sentences short, or that he avoid all detail and treat his subjects only in outline, but that every word tell.*[3]

There used to be a schoolroom exercise called 'writing the précis.' I gather from contact with many students that such old-fashioned discipline is no longer inflicted on them. This is to be regretted, for working at a précis is as valuable to a writer as *barre* exercises are to a dancer. Making a précis consisted simply of summing up the essential points of a paragraph in one sentence, a hard, hateful task that required much thinking. But its benefits remain, and those who have undergone this kind of drill may be grateful for the training when they have to hack a path through a jungle of prose to let in a little sunlight. The writer who is trained by the précis will not often let his own prose ramble about.

Even after an author has eliminated from his manuscript all the vestiges of his thesis which may appear as unnecessary repetition, notices, tables, listings, digressions, and the paraphernalia that belong in the appendix or back matter, and has squeezed out all unnecessary verbiage, he may find that he has still to cut further. Sometimes he has material for several off-shoot articles, and if he has a temperament that hates to waste anything, he can set this aside for future use and not feel that he has worked in vain.

Many writers of theses think of their job as merely the presentation of research and the results therefrom. Writers of books must get beyond the mere public display of data: they must chew the material well, digest it, and turn it into something of their own. Some of the signs of still undigested research are too many tables and graphs, an overabundance of footnotes, lengthy bibliographies, a rash of cross references, and excessive listing.

In certain books, of course, tables are important and necessary. Books in some areas of social science can hardly get along without them, and they are creeping more and more into historical studies, as the computer spews out statistical information historians have never been able to tap before. But tables and graphs mixed in with the text are often merely a resurgence of the thesis. At best, a table or chart interrupts the flow of the manuscript, and if the interruption is allowed, there should be an excellent reason.

If a table is short, the facts may often be summed up and incorporated into the text. If the table is long and the information is truly more easily grasped in tabular form, it can perhaps be removed to an appendix.

When an author has put in months or, more probably, years on his research, it is hard for him to give up any of it. He uses it all because it is at hand, just as some people climb mountains because they are there. That a table which is fruity with figures culled with indomitable patience from an out-of-the-way archive may be superfluous is not easy to accept. But this is a prime example of the shift in attitude from self to work necessary in transforming thesis to book. The author has to forget how much time, sweat, grant money, and eyestrain the table cost him. Now he thinks only of the book and its readers.

The same considerations apply to footnotes. An excessively footnoted text is obviously not the way to the hearts and minds of most readers. One of the principal differences between a thesis and a book is that more documentation is needed in a thesis, for the examiner must judge the value of the candidate's sources and how well he uses them. But when a book is opened out from a thesis, the reader assumes that the author's sources are reliable, at least until he is given reason for doubt. The sources should now sink beneath the surface for the most part. They are still there if anyone should challenge a statement, but they don't need to be quite so evident. Reader interest has shifted from research to interpretation, from the statements of others to the author's own, from the mining of the ore to the metal itself.

When pondering the reduction of notes, it is well to consider which category each fits into: is it a/ a citation, b/ a comment, c/ a cross-reference, or d/ an acknowledgement? The author should, of course, pin down direct quotations and acknowledge borrowings – comments are more difficult. Some footnotes fill in the picture and round out the text; some explain murky points that simply would take up too much room in the text; but others, although containing interesting information, are not absolutely vital. In general, explanatory notes are important but those that raise side issues are not. The process of cutting, eliminating, and paring may well include as many cross-references as possible, for they annoy the reader by requiring him to flip back and forth. Another reason to cut them out of the manuscript is the cost involved – and the possibility of errors in inserting the page numbers in page proof. If some cross-references must be used, it is well to make sure that 'see p. 14' is not just a casual remark but, if heeded, rewards the reader for his effort in looking it up.

The following page, culled from no book known to man, may serve as illustration:

Victor Krasovsky, better known inside and outside Russia by his pen-name, Karel Kopek, was born in a Uighur family in Sverdlovsk or somewhere in the Crimea in the year 1898.[1] Since Kopek's father was a premier danseur with the Bolshoi Ballet[2] and since we know that Kopek was brought up in Moscow,[3] we can consider him a Muscovite regardless of his place of birth. Kopek always thought of Moscow as his home; his fondness for this city is repeatedly expressed in his writings.[4]

Kopek's father was killed in 1900 when he crashed into the orchestra pit during a high leap.[5] The family, never very well off in any case, was now impoverished.[6] In 1909, at the age of 11, Kopek entered the Pavlovsk Elementary School on Bolotnaya Street.[7] At this school, he became friendly with a classmate, Nikolai Gorovdin, who was later to achieve great fame as an ornithologist,[8] and from whom we get an insight into Kopek's childhood and youth.[9] Kopek, moved no doubt by strong emotion, talks frankly of his school days in an article eulogizing Gorovdin at the time of his death. He said: 'For many years Gorovdin was my closest friend. We used to play hooky and go swimming in the Moskva together – we played darts – stole sweets from the local store. We lounged around on street corners and watched the girls go by. Occasionally we studied.'[10]

1 / There is some controversy about the date and place of Kopek's birth. Jonathan Larrabee in *Fifteen Hundred Modern Russian Short Stories* (Moscow, 1948), p. 84, mentions that Kopek was born in the Crimea in 1897. Arthur Field-Smythe in *A Short History of Russian Literature* (London, 1956) and the 'Note About the Author' at the end of Karel Kopek, *The Lazy Man's Donkey and Other Stories*, tr. Peter Twohig (New York, 1970), gives the date 1899 and the place Sverdlovsk. Phillip McGeoghan in *Modern Russian Fiction* (New Haven, 1971), p. 166, gives it as 1898 but provides no clue as to how he reached this date. I have calculated 1898 to be Kopek's year of birth from his article 'Russkoe Detstvo' in *Novaia Zhizn*, no. 1:23 (1959) in which he says that Gorovdin was a year younger than he. Gorovdin was born in 1899. Kopek also mentions that he left for Paris in 1924 when he was 26 years old. This also points to 1898 as his year of birth. Larrabee, Field-Smythe, and McGeoghan all agree that Kopek was born in the Crimea, but Heinegger in his chapter on early influences in *Der Symbolismus von Karel Kopek* states emphatically that he was born in Sverdlovsk and that his cradle is still there.

2 / See Zbigniew Morovski, *The Evolution of a Russian Writer* (Prague, 1963).

3 / Ibid., p. 24

4 / The most famous of his descriptions of Moscow is found in 'A City at Dawn,' but almost all of his novels are laid in that city and are full of vivid descriptions of the streets and the people.

5 / Morovski, p. 19

6 / It is difficult to comprehend what 'impoverishment' means in this context. Kopek first studied with a private tutor and then went to school and this can hardly be called a state of impoverishment but he repeatedly emphasizes his childhood poverty and later financial difficulties; in 1935 at the age of 37 he said: 'I have been poor since childhood.'

7 / I am indebted to Evgenii Narodny of Cochituate College for this information. Professor Narodny also attended the Pavlovsk School and remembers Kopek well, as a disagreeable individual given to spit balls and sarcastic remarks. Bolotnaya Street has since been renamed Marksistskaia.

8 / Nikolai Gorovdin became a professor at Kiev University and received many honorary degrees in Europe and America. He is the author of *An Encyclopedia of Ornithology* and about fifty other books on the subject as well as many treatises and articles. He was also renowned as a chess player.

9 / See Nikolai Gorovdin, *Some Memories of My Childhood*, tr. Laura Applegate (Boston, 1948).

10 / Karel Kopek, 'Nikolai Gorovdin,' *Sovetskii Mir* (June, 1965)

In a book these notes can certainly be reduced; they are excessive even for a thesis. The factual information about Kopek's early life need not be footnoted since the reader will assume that the writer has done his research. He is quite willing to accept the date of birth the writer puts forward and is not anxious to get embroiled in a controversy about it. Again, the writer's method and means of coming to a decision are not now as important as the decision itself. The remarks about whether or not Kopek was poor fall into the same category. We don't really need to know much about Gorovdin for the purposes of this book, although it could be interesting side-line information. It might be well to keep footnote 9 because Gorovdin's book appears to be the sole source of information on Kopek's childhood and could conceivably round out the reader's knowledge of the subject. A reference for the direct quotation (10) is, as noted, mandatory in scholarly writing.

Sometimes lengthy bibliographies also have to be pared. A bibliography enables the reader to carry on further research and can be a helpful part of the book. But the reader now being served may or may not desire to go into the subject thoroughly. In any event, this is not a list of all a candidate's research for the benefit of a committee of examiners; it is a list to help some readers find out more about the subject, and therefore need not include everything the author has read or everything that has ever been written on the subject.

The length and fullness of a bibliography in fact depend to a great extent upon the type of book. Whereas reduction of notes is nearly always advisable when turning a thesis into a book, bibliographies sometimes may not need trimming. Some bibliographies are pioneer work and are unavailable elsewhere; these obviously should be retained in their entirety. There are also varying degrees of selectivity in bibliographical material: some books are bibliographies in themselves. The author should look at his bibliography from the point of view of his reader, both the specialist and the general reader. What would a specialist need to point him to further research, and what would the general reader be likely to want? The shift here is, as in other matters, a shift in point of view. Just as an author anticipates in his index what his reader is apt to look for, so he anticipates in his bibliography what his reader might want to pursue. There should always be enough information to dispel any mystery about where the book or document can be found.

One more sign of undigested research is excessive listing, the firstly, secondly, thirdly habit which is halfway between tabular form and text. Such listing may be more of the outline showing through. Some attempt should be made to weave the material into the text. At any rate, if *a*, *b*, and *c* are used, avoid what Theodore M. Bernstein, in *The Careful Writer*, calls a 'bastard enumeration.' That is, if the list starts out with 1/ making an apple pie, the next item must not be 2/ the manufacture of a blueberry pie. A listing of proposed steps in a diplomatic crisis which begins with a/ denunciation of commercial treaty, should not switch to b/ advising women and children to leave, and end c/ withdraw financial aid. It should read a/ denunciation of the commercial treaty, b/ advice to women and children to leave, and c/ withdrawal of financial aid. The entries should be grammatically parallel, whatever form is used. Elementary? Very difficult to remember, actually – and forever turning up wrong in scholarly manuscripts.

Another point to remember about listing is that when an author has launched on a firstly, secondly, thirdly sequence, he should deliver promptly on his promises. It is disconcerting to come across 'the third school of thought' when the first two schools are several paragraphs away. Even an attentive reader tends to look back to make sure he and the author are both counting right. A multi-paragraph listing is often necessary, but when this happens the announcement of *a*, *b*, *c* should not be in the paragraph that contains a full treatment of only the first item in the list. This is another elementary – and frequent – error.

Headings and subheadings, too, are worth examining to see which should stay and which should not. Useful as they sometimes are, headings can also be the outline of the thesis showing through. Headings always have a text-book look. If the reader can be moved along without confusion simply by the text itself, headings should not be needed. But if a number of points of equal importance are being discussed headings may make it easier for the reader to remember them, and give him a convenient reference.

REPETITION

We all have a tendency to reiterate for emphasis – a self-defeating exercise because reiteration not only weakens the argument but obscures it. The effect is the same as that of using two adjectives where one will do. It seems as though two words ought to be twice as strong as one, but writing is not quantitative. Quality counts more than numbers.

Some authors use repetition deliberately to make sure their readers will not miss the point. But readers do not miss the implicit condescension. It is as if the author were saying: 'In case you missed this on the first round, here it is again. I didn't quite trust you to catch my meaning the first time.' We have again a crossover from the classroom technique of pampering the sleepy student.

Most repetition, however, is unintentional and could be eliminated. The author needs to step back and look at his work with some perspective, to let the manuscript gather a little dust, and then pick it up again. The repetition will then stand out.

One must beware particularly of repeating the same ideas in different words. An author will sometimes struggle to express his meaning in one sentence, then go on to the next where he tries a different combination of words to say the same thing instead of staying with the first sentence and making it clear. Whenever a writer comes across 'in other words' at the beginning of a sentence, he should pause and reflect. He may realize that he is repeating by restatement. Probably most repetition in manuscripts is a direct result of reluctance to revise one more time. We plod on, slogging through the mud of our own prose rather than taking the time to think of alternate routes and drier paths. For most of us, thinking is always harder than acting.

EXCESSIVE QUOTING

One of the first places to look for likely cuts in an overlong manuscript is in the quoted material. Quotations enliven a page but when a book is peppered with them, they look like padding, point to the author's unsureness, and become simply crutches to lean upon. The reader begins to suspect that the author is letting others do his work. Instead of using a full quotation, an author sometimes can achieve more by paraphrasing or perhaps by quoting only a characteristic or striking word or phrase. Before using a quotation, he should ask himself: Does it make a necessary point? Does it add concreteness? Does it explain what the author is talking about in fewer words?

We build upon one another's work. If we are struggling to make a necessary point, and someone else has explained it better, we should be concerned only with giving the reader the best possible break. Therefore, a quotation with (naturally) full credit, can be a means of clarification, a useful tool. The following quotation from H. W. Fowler should in this way make my point clearer and reinforce what I am saying: 'A writer expresses himself in words that have been used before because they give his meaning better than he can give it himself, or because they are beautiful or witty, or because he expects them to touch a chord of association in his reader or because he wishes to show that he is learned or well read. Quotations due to the last motive are invariably ill advised.'[4]

Using a quotation because it is 'beautiful or witty' may also be ill advised, especially in a scholarly work. Beauty has its dangers, as has wit. The two qualities can delude us into thinking that a quotation is apt or useful in context, when it is not. I remember a book on politics whose writer had fallen in love with Finley Peter Dunne's creation, Mr Dooley, and couldn't resist quoting him. I love Mr Dooley too, but he almost ran away with that book. He was, in this case, a nuisance and a diversion. The author finally compromised by using two short excerpts that made a point, concretely, wittily, enjoyably, humanly – but not overwhelmingly.

The second reason I have given for quoting, to add concreteness, is of particular importance in scholarly writing. By using direct quotation, an author can keep his book from becoming overly abstract and give the reader, even the most academic, some relief from the empyreal world of the intellectual concept. In a well-chosen quotation we mentally hear the speaker's voice and this silent echo adds an extra dimension to our understanding of the text. Such a direct quotation is always more forceful because the ideas have not been filtered through another person's mind.

In biography, of course, it is almost impossible to do without some of the subject's own words; at the least, omission of this made-to-order material would be a foolish waste. A stunning example of the skilful use of quotation is the following passage from Barbara Tuchman's *Stilwell and the American Experience in China*. Mrs Tuchman quoted General Stilwell in what she called 'one of the historic statements of the war.' He said: 'I claim we got a hell of a beating. We got run out of Burma and it is humiliating as hell.' The author added: 'The impact of the words was clean and hard. Stilwell's honesty cut through the pap and plush prose of Army public relations as the *San Francisco Chronicle* recalled at a later time, like a "sharp, salt wind."'[5]

There should be no need to point out that quoted matter should be accurate in every detail, but so many manuscripts are found faulty in this connection that it is worth reiterating. From an editorial point of view, the only changes that should be made in the quoted text are: 1/ an initial letter may be changed to a capital or a lower case letter, 2/ a final punctuation mark may be changed to make the quotation fit into the syntax of the text. Otherwise, wording, spelling, capitalization, and the punctuation of the original must be kept intact. According to the Chicago *Manual*:

> In a passage from a modern book, journal, or newspaper an obvious typographical error may be silently corrected, but in a passage from an

*older work or from a manuscript source any idiosyncrasy of spelling
should be observed. In quoting from older works an author may consider
it desirable to modernize spelling and punctuation for the sake of clarity.
When he does this, he should so inform the reader, either in a footnote or,
in a book containing many such quotations, by a general statement in the
preface or elsewhere.*[6]

Some authors quote to such excess that they seem to be trying to save their
readers a trip to the library. One young student thought he was doing the
reader a service when, instead of giving a mere reference in a footnote, he
provided great chunks of his sources word for word. This kind of generosity
is bound to annoy a reader who is quite capable of looking up references if
he wants to, unless, perhaps, the books are hidden away in a Tibetan monastery. With the advent of information-retrieval services, lengthy quoting
will be even less desirable: if sources are at the other end of a pushbutton,
there is hardly any need to print excerpts. Then, perhaps, we shall see the
day when the quotation as crutch will be virtually useless and scholars will be
more inclined to manufacture their own beauty and wit and all by themselves
find the apt words to express their meaning.

PERMISSIONS

While we are on the subject of quotations, a word about permissions might
be useful.

Permission to use a quotation in a thesis does not cover its use in a published
work. A thesis writer may feel he has done all that is necessary if he has a
friendly letter from Lord Pricklypear authorizing him to dip into his family
archives. He and his publisher may have a rude awakening when they discover that the generous earl's Aunt Agatha is suing for half a million dollars.
Although most cases are not so shattering, books have been recalled from
bookstores for just such reasons, and much money and sleep have been lost
all around.

In the case of unpublished material (letters, for instance), it is also not
enough to obtain permission from the library where such material has been
deposited; permission must also be secured from the owner or from his estate.
The writer of a letter (or his heirs or assigns) is the copyright owner. It is
always best to track him down, even if it takes time and patience, and get him
or his heir to write another letter for your publisher's files giving you iron-

clad permission. In the United Kingdom, however, a scholar is allowed (since 1956) to reproduce any unpublished manuscript or copy of one which is open to public inspection in a library or museum, after 50 years from the death of the author and 100 after creation of the work.

Usually it is not worth while to expend much effort to secure permission for the use of copyright material until the manuscript has been accepted by a publisher, since most publishers will not handle requests for permission unless the author furnishes the name of the house that will be issuing his book. In addition, the publisher will advise the author whether applications are required – in many cases, the application of the clause in the copyright law covering fair use or fair dealing makes requests unnecessary, but publishers differ in their views about it – and he may have stipulations to make about market rights which should be incorporated in such requests. Needless to say, because of the extra trouble involved, the inclusion of a large number of long quotations from copyright works does not add to the attractiveness of a manuscript in the eyes of a prospective publisher.

It would also be unwise to begin to transform a thesis on a modern author into a book in which there is extensive quoting from his works, without first inquiring from the author's publisher or agent whether permission is likely to be given. Such an enquiry has the added value of just possibly interesting the original publisher in the study himself, or of producing a warning that someone else has pre-empted the topic.

1 / Henry David Thoreau, *Walden and Other Writings* (New York: Bantam Books, 1962). Introduction by Joseph Wood Krutch, p. 21

2 / Wilson Follett, *Modern American Usage: A Guide* (New York: Hill & Wang, 1966), p. 14

3 / William Strunk, Jr., and E.B. White, *The Elements of Style* (New York: The Macmillan Company, 1972), p. 69

4 / H.W. Fowler, *A Dictionary of Modern English Usage*, 2nd ed. rev. by Sir Ernest Gowers (New York: Oxford University Press, 1965), s.v. 'Quotation'

5 / Barbara Tuchman, *Stilwell and the American Experience in China, 1911–1945* (New York: The Macmillan Company, 1970), p. 300

6 / *A Manual of Style*, 12th ed. rev. (Chicago: University of Chicago Press, 1969)

Thesis to book: what to do with what is left

OLIVE HOLMES

Once the signs of a thesis have been eliminated, the author should have a manuscript that he can begin to work with and shape into a book. The first step in this more positive process is to decide how much background information his new readers will need. This is rarely easy, for the readers' knowledge will vary from subject to subject and also from time to time. The high school student of today, for example, is far more knowledgeable in certain areas (particularly scientific ones) than his counterpart of some years ago. There is a well-known maxim that can be adapted to these circumstances: never underestimate the intelligence of a reader, and never overestimate his knowledge.

To create a self-contained book the author has to try to put himself in the reader's skin. He must perform an act of imagination and of perception that is not required of the thesis writer. A scholar engrossed in his own specialty does not find it easy to think beyond it to communicate with others who do not have the same knowledge. Even in everyday communication, we tend to assume either that a person has no need of explanation or that our subject must be explained to death. Those who learn to fill others' gaps without condescension, offering just as much as the others want to know, but no more, develop a skill that is as useful in everyday life as it is on the printed page. It is particularly useful, of course, for a teacher or parent. It is related to the ability to listen selectively.

Every book has a context which can enrich and deepen its meaning and add to its interest. The fragmentary piece of life captured in print is never the whole story. And although focus is essential, paradoxically a book is made more self-contained by enlarging its horizons. When Harvey Cox began *The Feast of Fools* with an 'Overture' in which he gave the history of the medieval Feast of Fools, he said: 'This is not a historical treatise and I recall the Feast of Fools only as a symbol of the subject of this book.'[1] But it *is* important background material for an understanding of his theme. Garrett Mattingly gave his readers an entire panorama of Europe in the fifteenth century in four pages in *Catherine of Aragon*, a fine piece of background writing, imparting a feeling of the times without too many bewildering figures and events.[2] Margaret Mead's sweeping introduction to *Culture and Commitment* placed her theme in the wide context of twentieth-century culture:

> *An essential and extraordinary aspect of man's present state is that, at this moment in which we are approaching a world-wide culture and the possibility of becoming fully aware citizens of the world in the late twentieth century, we have simultaneously available to us for the first time examples of the ways men have lived at every period over the last fifty thousand years ... At the time that a New Guinea native looks at a pile of yams and pronounces them 'a lot' because he cannot count them, teams at Cape Kennedy calculate the precise second when an Apollo mission must change its course if it is to orbit around the moon. This is a situation that has never occurred before in human history.*[3]

With this preparation we are ready for the author's first chapter which begins: 'The distinctions I am making among three different kinds of culture ... are a reflection of the period in which we live.'[4] Since Mead has already given us a ten-page review of the period in which we live, what she says in the course of the book is readily understood.

In deciding what kind of background will prepare his thesis for its opening out into a book, a young scholar might find it helpful to read a number of introductions to scholarly books in fields other than his own. A friend who has no knowledge whatsoever of the field also may be able to provide valuable advice, if he reads the opening chapter and specifies what kind of information he needs to understand it.

After an author has decided how much and what kind of background material to present, there remains the question of where to put it. A large lump of background usually stalls the forward movement of a manuscript; therefore, if much background must be given all at once, it is best to put it near the beginning. The most difficult but the most effective way to provide the reader with background information is to give it in small quantities at a time and as needed.

Some background can be introduced by simply explaining briefly when an unknown name or term crops up. In the following quotation from a book about Rabindranath Tagore, the author weaves in his background skilfully (250 pages along in the text):

> *The opening decades of the twentieth century brought major political changes to the Hindu-British relationship in Bengal, and therefore to Tagore's position in his own province. The spread of English education and consequently of English political ideals had by 1900 produced a large and vocal school of moderate nationalists. The British bureaucracy, led by the conservative Lord Curzon from 1898 to 1905, looked down on this Anglicized class as a deracinated minority, and grievously affronted it by partitioning Bengal in 1905 into Hindu and Muslim majority areas. The ensuing anti-British agitation ... produced a new extremist school of nationalists who rejected both British rule and British influence on Indian culture. Tagore parted company with the extremists, and was regarded by them as a defector.[5]*

The ins and outs of Hindu-British relationships in Bengal are not known to most of us and at this point in the narrative even specialists may need a reminder of the climate in which Tagore worked. But the author has not left Tagore on the sidelines while interjecting a little British and Indian history. He has kept him close by and pulled him back into the paragraph, keeping us aware that Tagore is the central figure moving against the historical landscape. This background does not slow down the text but deepens and enhances it.

The author may, of course, have provided such background in his thesis, but his new readers probably need a fuller briefing than his doctoral committee. If he gives them the right amount in the right place, he will have taken a long step toward involving his audience and creating a self-contained book.

Clarity is an editor's touchstone, an author's goal. There is no communication without it, and so it becomes an absolute first in any consideration of style. Often the impediment to clarity is not inability to express a thought so much as inability to think clearly. Much bad writing comes from the belief that writing and thinking are disparate activities. Although it is possible that a man can think well but not be able to write well, and that writing can seem facile and clear even if there is not much thought behind it, the best writing is usually an ideal marriage of thought and word. Obscurity can be the result of a brain working so fast that words come out in a bewildering avalanche, but confused sentences are far more likely to be the result of muddleheadedness. It is more pleasant, of course, to believe that one's brain is working too fast than that it is muddled. Ambrose Bierce said 'Good writing ... is clear thinking made visible.'[6] 'Let the meaning choose the word, and not the other way about,' was George Orwell's sound advice.[7]

The teaching of English as grammar has implanted the wrong order in our minds. The average teacher of English 'appears to attempt to place the emphasis upon writing rather than writing-about-something-for-someone.'[8] As a result we tend to think first of words (this is where all the high-sounding pomposity comes from) rather than meanings. We become overawed by mere symbols when we should be paying attention to realities.

Thinking is not always a verbal type of cerebration. There is some evidence that the wordless half of the brain could help us in getting words on paper if we would only let it. Perhaps a lively liaison between the two halves of the brain is indeed the source of great writing. Orwell's advice to put off using words as long as possible and first to 'get one's meaning as clear as one can through pictures or sensations'[9] seems to bear this out, and we know that Einstein used both halves with superlative ease.

When Einstein was asked how he arrived at some of his most original ideas, he explained the he rarely thought in words at all. 'A thought comes, and I may try to express it in words afterwards,' he said. His concepts first appeared through 'physical entities' – certain signs and more or less clear images that he could reproduce and combine. These elements were 'of visual and some of muscular type,' he added. 'Conventional words or other signs have to be sought for laboriously only in a secondary stage, when the mentioned associative play is sufficiently established and can be reproduced at will.'[10]

However the author's own mind works, it is he who stands between the reader and confusion. I once wrote on the margin of a manuscript: 'This paragraph is very confusing.' The author replied: 'But the situation was confused.' My reply was: 'Keep your head when all about you are losing theirs.'

The way to achieve clarity, therefore, is to be precise, first in thought, then in expression. Truth of expression corresponds to scholarly truth: exactness of language comes from honesty, patient searching, and a refusal to settle for second best. This kind of truth should be as important to the scholar as the exactness of his thoughts. There is 'a lie of the approximate word,' as Grace Paley puts it, as well as a lie of 'the brilliant sentence you love the most.'[11] Morris Philipson, director of the University of Chicago Press, has commented: 'The most significant purpose of language [is] communication between people – or, ideally, communion among people ... What is execrable is what misleads, what traduces, what injects error, what cloaks the absence of thought or feeling, what pretends to be something other than it is, what is false.'[12] When a man matches his words and deeds, he is said to have integrity, or wholeness. His writing has integrity when he matches his words and thoughts.

ABSTRACTIONS

In seeking clarity, the scholarly writer faces the major problem of trying to present abstract ideas to his reader. Human nature tends to reject the vague and the general in favour of the specific and the concrete. Consequently, the writer must somehow bring his abstractions down to earth.

The problem in dealing clearly with abstract ideas occurs because thinking comes before words. As George Orwell explained it: 'When you think of a concrete object, you think wordlessly and then, if you want to describe the thing you have been visualizing you probably hunt about till you find the exact words that seem to fit it. When you think of something abstract you are more inclined to use words from the start, and unless you make a conscious effort to prevent it, the existing dialect will come rushing in and do the job for you, at the expense of blurring or even changing your meaning.'[13]

This 'existing dialect' is the enemy; its use leads to pale, dull, cliché-ridden, and incomprehensible prose. It leads away from rather than toward communication.

William Howells in *Back of History* handled the abstract word 'culture' by using homely detail. He ended one paragraph: 'Culture is all those things that are *not* inherited biologically,' and began the next: 'Instead, culture consists of everything that has ever been accepted as a way of doing or thinking, and so taught by one person to another.' But he was still speaking in general terms, so after an explanation of teaching and learning he narrowed down: 'Let us take some simple examples from what would be a very simple culture. A digging stick of a particular kind, for digging up wild vegetables for food, is culture. So is using a skin for keeping warm. So is the idea of appointing a war chief for the group, or the idea of marriage.'[14]

When writing about abstract ideas, we tend to classify rather than describe. A good point to remember is that scientific language classifies; and all writers are affected by the popularity of science and the vogue for using scientific terms. But there is more reality in a blade of grass than in the concept of chlorophyll. We may learn how to categorize the fishes but forget how a fresh-caught mackerel tastes. We may know the names of birds, families, and species, but be deaf to their songs. So the addiction to the scientific term has its dangers, and one of them is a deadening effect upon writing and speaking. The more technical we get, the more we use the interchangeable, standardized parts of technical language, and neglect concrete, sensual description.

The writer of the following has been more than ordinarily affected by 'scientism,' as Wilson Follett calls this kind of language: 'This aspect was, of course, more significant in terms of personalized, individual relationships. Another aspect of relations, not less affected by personal factors was dealt with, however, as an institutional problem.'[15]

Contrast that uncertain paragraph with this one whose author described rather than classified, worked from the particular to the general, and gave first the evidence of the senses:

> It is interesting to contemplate a tangled bank, clothed with many plants of many kinds, with birds singing on the bushes, with various insects flitting about, and with worms crawling through the damp earth, and to reflect that these elaborately constructed forms, so different from each

79

*other, and dependent upon each other in so complex a manner, have all
been produced by laws acting upon us. These laws taken in the largest
sense, being Growth with Reproduction; Inheritance ... Variability ...
Ratio of Increase so high as to lead to a Struggle for Life ... Natural
Selection ... Divergence of Character and the Extinction of less-im-
proved forms.*[16]

This is an excerpt from the final paragraph of Darwin's *Origin of Species* – a
book that seems to have communicated its message to the world.

John Dewey in his essay, 'The Influence of Darwinism on Philosophy,'
told some of that story:

*The conceptions that had reigned in the philosophy of nature and
knowledge for two thousand years, the conceptions that had become the
familiar furniture of the mind, rested on the assumption of the superiority
of the fixed and final ... In laying hands upon the sacred ark of absolute
permanency ... the 'Origin of Species' introduced a mode of thinking that
... was bound to transform the logic of knowledge.*[17]

Dewey himself pinned down the general by using particular terms: 'familiar
furniture of the mind' and 'sacred ark of absolute permanency.'

Using metaphor or analogy, as in the above passages, is one way of
making abstractions more understandable. Introducing people into the text
is another. Alfred North Whitehead, in discussing the conflict between
religion and science, told how early theologians 'deduced from the Bible
opinions concerning the nature of the physical universe.' He not only gave a
specific illustration of this statement but introduced a character:

In the year A.D. *535, a monk named Cosmas wrote a book which he
entitled* Christian Topography. *He was a travelled man who had visited
India and Ethiopia; and finally he lived in a monastery at Alexandria,
which was then a great centre of culture. In this book, basing himself upon
the direct meaning of Biblical texts as construed by him in a literal
fashion, he denied the existence of the antipodes, and asserted that the
world is a flat parallelogram whose length is double its breadth.*[18]

Here is not only an idea but the man who held the idea; the idea becomes
more memorable because we know something about the man.

'Good writing,' according to John K. Galbraith, 'and this is especially important in a subject such as economics, must also involve the reader in the matter at hand. It is not enough to explain. The images that are in the mind of the writer must be made to reappear in the mind of the reader, and it is the absence of this ability that causes much economic writing to be condemned, quite properly, as abstract.'[19]

Totalitarian jargon (whether Communist or Fascist) is a conspicuous modern phenomenon which can smother the thoughts of scholars as well as adherents in the grey dust of easy abstractions. 'Collectivization,' 'cadres,' 'rectification,' and that horror, 'co-operativization,' are all examples of words of category rather than of description. These heavy nouns are, according to Barzun, 'static and inclusive' phrases:

> they deny the doer and replace him by an activity, a process (a favorite word) which is therefore unchanging, eternal, and which gives the user the sense of being 'scientific' through 'covering' the events by abstraction ... This sort of writing, easy to write and dull to read, is the surest protection against the critical analysis of thought. It sounds as if its meaning were not only lucid but important, for example: 'This is undertaken in the context of comprehensive patient care and includes theory and supervised practice related to the assumption of a leadership role.' Who is doing what? No one; nothing. This part of a nurse's training has been lifted from the world of bedpans and wrinkled sheets to the abode where the eternal abstractions are.[20]

What happens ultimately when a concept is left in the 'abode of eternal abstractions' and not brought down to earth where the human mind can understand it is grimly illustrated in the explanation given by Lieutenant William Calley, during his trial for killing civilians at My Lai: 'When my troops were getting massacred and mauled by an enemy I couldn't see, I couldn't feel and I couldn't touch,' he explained, 'nobody in the military ever described them as anything other than Communism ... They didn't give it a race, they didn't give it a sex, they didn't give it an age. They never let me believe it was just a philosophy in a man's mind. That was my enemy out there.'[21]

Abstract words, when they move too far away from humanity and reality, can even kill.

Pace, or rhythm, is another factor in good writing. Pace helps to produce the forward movement necessary to hold the reader's interest and to avoid 'the slow, pedantic crawl of scholarly prose,' in Edwin O. Reischauer's phrase.

The analogy of the drama is helpful. Pace is an exceedingly important ingredient in the production of any play and to set it is a part of a director's job. Comedy is played at a fast pace; tragedy is slower. But whatever the pace is, it is not accidental.

Although the reader may not be aware of this quality in a straightforward piece of expository writing, it exists, and it is established by the author. The passages that lag, the ones that are redundant, the words that slow down and impede the flow of thought, diminish the pace and make a piece of writing static and lifeless.

The elimination of unnecessary words is one way to achieve forward movement. The use of active verbs is another. The third step is a matter of ear, of listening to one's own words – reading aloud perhaps, but in any case listening. A perfectly clear and perfectly grammatical sentence can still grate on the ear. We all have prose rhythms that we prefer, not only through habit, but no doubt by character and temperament. And since writing is individual or nothing, we tend to use these rhythms as we write. This inner rhythm is a vital ingredient of style. We learn a lot about ourselves when we discover what kind of pace we prefer. P. G. Wodehouse darts at a fast bicycle clip; Winston Churchill rolls like a ship; E. B. White strolls but never meanders from the path.

Pace is strongly affected by word order. A simple change in the order of words can not only alter the meaning of a sentence completely but speed it up or slow it down. On a grander scale, the organization of the manuscript as a whole affects the pace. The old Aristotelian beginning, middle, and end construction is still valid and the magic number three (the three acts of a play, for instance) in some mysterious way satisfies a deep psychological instinct and works well.

Beginnings and endings require watching and working over. The first and last words of sentences, the first and last sentences of paragraphs, the first and last paragraphs of chapters, the first and last chapters of a manuscript, linger longest in the reader's mind and should be the strongest points. Nothing should waver at the beginning or peter out at the end. The last half of the last sentence of the concluding chapter of *The Origin of Species* reads: '...

whilst this planet has gone cycling on according to the fixed law of gravity, from so simple a beginning endless forms most beautiful and most wonderful have been, and are being evolved.'[22] How much less effective this last sentence would have been if Darwin had written 'Endless forms ... are being evolved whilst this planet has gone cycling on according to the fixed law of gravity.' It cannot be accidental that he ended with the theme of evolution.

In organizing the pace and structure of a book, a sense of story is often helpful. William Howells said that he 'tried to make a single story of the human background' in *Back of History*.[23] Many a manuscript has been un-snarled by giving it a simple chronological sequence which is actually a kind of story line. For any sequence of ideas, development of an argument, or pursuit of research, there is a natural structure which, once found, enables a reader to follow more easily and with greater interest than if the facts are merely strung one after the other like beads. There is still in all of us an atavistic memory of the technique of the story told around the campfire.

A reader will continue to follow if he feels he is going somewhere, deepening his insight, satisfying his curiosity, or extending his knowledge, but if he has to stand still or go in circles, he may become bored. 'Build,' a technical term used in the drama to describe the way in which a scene or a play builds up to a climax, thus can also be applied to the forward movement within a manuscript – as a whole, by chapter, or in the smaller units of sentence and paragraph.

AUTHORS AND EDITORS

When an author turns a thesis into a book, he is often working with an editor for the first time, and is not quite sure what to expect. His editor will probably turn out to be a person who, oddly enough, is just as interested as he is in producing a good book and who stands ready with a blue pencil to unravel tangled sentences, see to it that commas and capitals are in the right places, pick up loose ends, weed the unwanted words, passive verbs, and infelicitous metaphors, and get across the idea that even if things are not quite right, they can be fixed.

It may sometimes seem to an author that an editor takes an occupational delight in finding flaws. Yet the editor would be of little use if she (or he – but there are a lot of women editors) did not scrutinize his manuscript and occasionally suggest the removal of a crenellated turret here and there from his dream castle, or the addition of a stronger arch. Nevertheless the author remains in full control of his own work. It is his privilege to reject editorial advice, although he may be foolish to do so. If he has doubts whether a particular word should be used, or a particular sentence recast, or a section cut out, he should find out exactly why the editor recommends such a move. It is up to the editor to explain satisfactorily, and the author should present his own point of view if he differs. This kind of dialogue is necessary, not for the peace of mind of either author or editor, but for the sake of the book. An editor does not and cannot be expected to have the same grasp of subject matter as the author, and the author may not have the same grasp of print or understanding of the reader's needs. Therefore, many points often have to be threshed out. But the final decision belongs, as a matter of course, to the author.

A good editor will also give an author confidence in his own powers. Research and writing are lonely occupations. It is easy to become discouraged in solitary confinement. The mere human contact with another mind, particularly one that is not competitive but is as eager as the author to make the jumble into a good book, can be encouraging. Most editors are careful of an author's feelings and alert to his good points. They can often give him hope that there is a way out of the morass. They have doubtless seen far worse manuscripts and their range of experience, like the doctor's (which gives a patient confidence simply because he has seen everything), can make an author feel that he does not have a candidate for the worst book of the year, but indeed a pretty good one that can be made better, can perhaps even be made into a fine one. This psychological lift can be an important ingredient in the making of a book.

Creating anything is like holding a bird in the hand. Hold it too tightly and it will be hurt and never fly; hold it too loosely and it will escape too soon. An editor's job is to show the author how to clasp and unclasp that hand, so his ideas may fly on strong wings.

1/ Harvey Cox, *The Feast of Fools* (Cambridge, Mass.: Harvard University Press, 1969)
2/ Garrett Mattingly, *Catherine of Aragon* (Boston: Little, Brown & Co., 1941), pp. 3-7
3/ Margaret Mead, *Culture and Commitment: A Study of the Generation Gap*

(Garden City, N.Y.: Doubleday & Co., Inc., 1970), p. xv

4/ *Ibid.*, p. 1

5/ Stephen N. Hay, *Asian Ideas of East and West: Tagore and His Critics in Japan, China, and India* (Cambridge, Mass.: Harvard University Press, 1970)

6/ Ambrose Bierce, *Write It Right: A Little Blacklist of Literary Faults* (New York and Washington: Meale Publishing Co., 1909)

7/ George Orwell, 'Politics and the English Language,' in *Shooting an Elephant and Other Essays* (London: Secker and Warburg, 1950), p. 100

8/ Wendell Johnson, 'You Can't Write Writing,' in *The Use and Misuse of Language*, ed. S. I. Hayakawa (Greenwich, Conn.: Fawcett Publications, Inc., 1962)

9/ Orwell, 'Politics and the English Language,' pp. 99, 100

10/ Maya Pines, 'We Are Left-Brained or Right-Brained,' *New York Times Magazine* (9 September 1973)

11/ Grace Paley, 'Some Notes on Teaching: Probably Spoken,' in Jonathan Baumbach, ed., *Writers as Teachers: Teachers as Writers* (New York: Holt, Rinehart and Winston, 1970)

12/ Morris Philipson, Foreword to Jacques Barzun, *On Writing, Editing, and Publishing* (Chicago: University of Chicago Press, 1971)

13/ Orwell, 'Politics and the English Language,' p. 100

14/ William Howells, *Back of History: The Story of Our Own Origins* (Garden City, N.Y.: Doubleday & Co., Inc., 1954); paperback edition, Natural History Library rev. ed., 1963

15/ Wilson Follett, *Modern American Usage: A Guide* (New York: Hill & Wang, 1966), s.v. 'Scientism'

16/ Charles Darwin, *Origin of Species* (New York: D. Appleton & Co., 1860), pp. 423-4

17/ John Dewey, *The Influence of Darwinism on Philosophy and Other Essays* (New York: Henry Holt & Co., Inc., 1910)

18/ Alfred North Whitehead, *Science and the Modern World* (New York: The Macmillan Company, 1925)

19/ John K. Galbraith, 'The Language of Economics,' *Economics, Peace, and Laughter* (Boston: Houghton Mifflin Company, 1971), p. 29

20/ Jacques Barzun, 'The Language of Learning and Pedantry,' *The House of Intellect* (New York: Harper & Brothers, 1959), p. 233

21/ *The New York Times* (23 February, 1971)

22/ Darwin, *Origin of Species*, pp. 416, 424

23/ Howells, *Back of History*, p. 361

Index